Genre Expository

Essential Question
How are people able to fly?

The Future of Flight

by Anna Harris

Chapter 1

Where to from Here?

People have imagined all kinds of strange spaceships.

Have you ever seen a movie that is set in the future? You may have seen people in flying cars. People may have been traveling to other planets in spaceships. Could these movies show air and space travel of the future?

Imagine it is now 2040. You need to get to the store. How will you get there? You might fly there with a jetpack.

People have already **built** some jetpacks. One jetpack can make a **flight** for 30 minutes. The driver uses two joysticks to guide the **direction** of the jetpack.

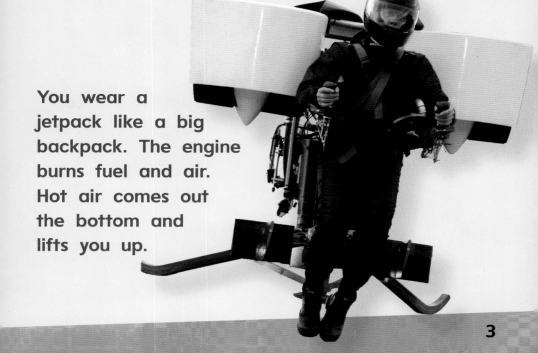

You wear a jetpack like a big backpack. The engine burns fuel and air. Hot air comes out the bottom and lifts you up.

Experts don't think that jetpacks will work well for small trips. So scientists are studying very small aircraft. The aircraft could be like small flying cars. People would use them for short trips.

This picture shows what a small aircraft might look like.

The inside of this aircraft looks like the inside of a car.

Scientists are planning how this aircraft would work. It would be **controlled** by a computer. People would choose where they want to go. The aircraft would fly there. The aircraft would send out signals to other aircraft. This would stop them from crashing into each other.

STOP AND CHECK

What is one kind of aircraft you learned about in this chapter?

Chapter 2

Around the World

NASA has built this super-fast aircraft.

Today, most **passenger** jets travel at 500 to 600 miles per hour. Scientists are working on planes that can go much faster.

NASA has built a very fast aircraft. It has a new kind of engine, called a **scramjet engine**. The aircraft has no pilot. A computer controls it. Its top speed is 7,000 miles per hour!

One company has bigger plans for a new passenger jet. It will travel at 3,000 miles per hour. Today it takes 12 hours to fly from London to Tokyo. The new plane will take just two hours!

How High They Fly

Future passenger jet 20 miles high

Boeing 747 6 miles high

The new jet will use three kinds of engines. One will be a jet engine. The second will be a **rocket engine.** The third will be a scramjet engine. This jet won't **pollute** as much as other airplanes do. However, it won't be ready until 2050.

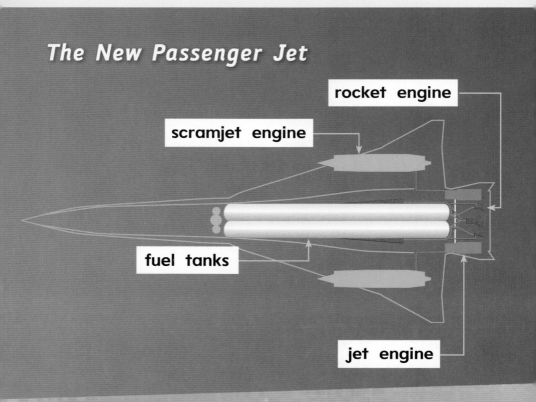

The New Passenger Jet

rocket engine

scramjet engine

fuel tanks

jet engine

Traveling Around the World

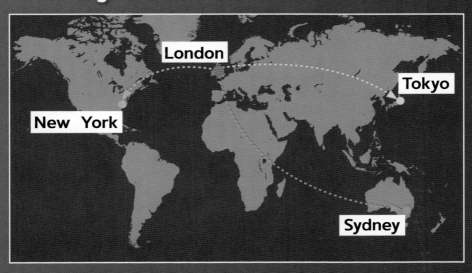

TRAVEL TIMES TODAY

London to New York	7 hours
London to Tokyo, Japan	12 hours
London to Sydney, Australia	23 hours

TRAVEL TIMES IN THE FUTURE

London to New York	1 hour
London to Tokyo, Japan	2 hours
London to Sydney, Australia	3.5 hours

STOP AND CHECK

What might passenger jets be like in the future?

9

Chapter 3

Traveling into Space

Today, astronauts travel into space. They are **launched** on rocket ships. They travel to the International Space Station. The space station is in **orbit** around Earth.

These astronauts are at the International Space Station.

Now a company has built a new spaceship. It will take passengers into space. The spaceship hasn't gone into space yet. It has been on test flights.

This spaceship needs help to get up. A special plane will lift it high into the sky. Then the plane will let it go. Rocket engines will fire up. The spaceship will blast into space. Later, it will use its wings to **glide** back to the ground.

The plane and the spaceship are on a test flight. The spaceship is in the middle.

These people are testing out a model of the spaceship.

Each flight will take two and a half hours. The spaceship will travel 68 miles above Earth. There is less **gravity** the farther an object is from Earth. Passengers will **float** inside the plane for five minutes.

The flights are **popular**. Many people have bought tickets. One ticket costs $200,000.

People have been exploring new places for a long time. They have built clever **machines** to travel faster and farther. Some ideas in this book might seem **impossible**. But who knows what will happen in the future?

Could people land on Mars one day?

STOP AND CHECK

What will the flights be like on the spaceship?

How to Make a Balloon Hovercraft

What You Need:

pop-top lid
from drink bottle

craft glue

old CD

balloon

craft glue

What to Do:

1. Glue the bottom of the lid over the hole in the CD.

2. Close the lid. Let the glue dry overnight.

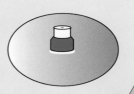

3. Blow up the balloon. Hold the neck so that no air escapes.

4. Stretch the neck of the balloon over the lid. Now your balloon hovercraft is done!

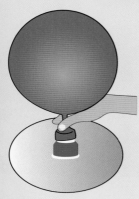

Respond to Reading

Summarize

How might air travel change? Use details from *The Future of Flight* to summarize. Your chart may help you.

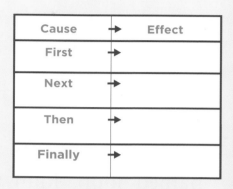

Cause	→	Effect
First	→	
Next	→	
Then	→	
Finally	→	

Text Evidence

1. Reread page 3. What happens when fuel and air are burned in the jetpack engine? Cause and Effect

2. Find the word *escapes* on page 14. What does it mean? What clues help you figure it out? Vocabulary

3. Write about why people build new aircraft. How might future air travel affect people? Write About Reading

Compare Texts
Read about how a Norse god
could fly.

The
Cloak of Feathers

Once, there was a goddess of youth
named Idun. Idun took care of the magic
apples. The apples let the gods live forever.

One day, a giant captured Idun. The
giant could change into anything he
wanted. He became an eagle. He carried
Idun away. The gods grew old without
the apples.

The gods had to rescue Idun. A woman named Freya had a special cloak, which was made of feathers from a falcon. Anyone wearing the cloak could change into a bird.

The god Loki borrowed the cloak. He turned into a falcon in one quick **motion**. He found Idun. He changed her into a nut so he could carry her in his claws. Then Loki saw that the giant had become an eagle. The eagle was chasing him!

Loki finally made it home. The gods lit fires on top of the city walls. The eagle's wings caught fire when it tried to get over the walls. It had to fly to the ocean to put out the flames. The gods had won.

Idun changed back into a goddess. She gave apples to all the gods. Soon they looked young again!

 Make Connections

How was the god Loki able to fly?
Essential Question

We have aircraft that allow us to fly. Why would people make up stories about using magic to fly? Text to Text

Glossary

gravity *(GRAV-i-tee)* the force that pulls objects toward Earth *(page 12)*

orbit *(AWR-buht)* the path an object takes as it moves around another object *(page 10)*

rocket engine *(ROK-it EN-juhn)* an engine that burns fuel and oxygen to create thrust *(page 8)*

scramjet engine *(SKRAM-jet EN-juhn)* an engine that has no moving parts and is built for very fast speeds *(page 6)*

Index

Focus on
Science

Purpose To find out about motion.

What to Do

Step 1 Make a hovercraft by following the instructions on page 14.

Step 2 Put the hovercraft on a desk and push it. How far does it move?

Step 3 Open the pop-top lid and push the hovercraft. How far does it move this time?

Step 4 Change the size of the balloon. Write what you think will happen.

Conclusion What did you learn from this experiment?

Chapter 2

DR. KEN BLANCHARD

David E. Wright (Wright)

Few people have created a positive impact on the day-to-day management of people and companies more than Dr. Kenneth Blanchard, who is known around the world simply as Ken, a prominent, gregarious, sought-after author, speaker, and business consultant. Ken is universally characterized by friends, colleagues, and clients as one of the most insightful, powerful, and compassionate men in business today. Ken's impact as a writer is far-reaching. His phenomenal bestselling book, *The One Minute Manager®*, co-authored with Spencer Johnson, has sold more than thirteen million copies worldwide and has been translated into more than twenty-five languages. Ken is Chairman and Chief Spiritual Officer of the Ken Blanchard Companies. The organization's focus is to energize organizations around the world with customized training in bottom line business strategies based on the simple, yet powerful principles inspired by Ken's bestselling books.

Dr. Blanchard, welcome to *Speaking of Success*!

Dr. Ken Blanchard (Blanchard)
Well, it's nice to talk to you, David. It's good to be here.

Wright
I must tell you that preparing for your interview took quite a bit more time than usual. The scope of your life's work and your business, the Ken Blanchard Companies, would make for a dozen fascinating interviews. Before we dive into the specifics of some of your projects and strategies, will you give our readers a brief synopsis of your life—how you came to be the Ken Blanchard we all know and respect?

Blanchard
Well, I'll tell you, David, I think life is what you do when you are planning on doing something else. I think that was John Lennon's line. I never intended to do what I have been doing. In fact, all my professors in college told me that I couldn't write. I wanted to do college work, which I did, and they said, "You had better be an administrator." So I decided I was going to be a Dean of Students. I got provisionally accepted into my master's degree program and then provisionally accepted at Cornell, because I never could take any of those standardized tests.

I took the college boards four times and finally got 502 in English. I don't have a test-taking mind. I ended up in a university in Athens, Ohio, in 1966 as an Administrative Assistant to the Dean of the Business School. When I got there he said, "Ken, I want you to teach a course. I want all my deans to teach." I had never thought about teaching because they said I couldn't write, and teachers had to publish. He put me in the manager's department.

I've taken enough bad courses in my day and I wasn't going to teach one. I really prepared and had a wonderful time with the students. I was chosen as one of the top ten teachers on the campus coming out of the chute!

I just had a marvelous time. A colleague by the name of Paul Hersey was chairman of the management department. He wasn't very friendly to me initially because the Dean had led me into his department, but I heard he was a great teacher. He taught organizational behavior and leadership. So I said, "Can I sit in on your course next semester?"

"Nobody audits my courses," he said. "If you want to take it for credit, you're welcome."

I couldn't believe it. I had a doctoral degree and he wanted me to take his course for credit, so I signed up.

The registrar didn't know what to do with me because I already had a doctorate, but I wrote the papers and took the course, and it was great.

In June 1967, Hersey came into my office and said, "Ken, I've been teaching in this field for ten years. I think I'm better than anybody, but I can't write. I'm a nervous wreck, and I'd love to write a textbook with somebody. Would you write one with me?"

I said, "We ought to be a great team. You can't write and I'm not supposed to be able to, so let's do it!"

Thus began this great career of writing and teaching. We wrote a textbook called *Management of Organizational Behavior: Utilizing Human Resources.* It came out in its eighth edition October 3, 2000 and the nineth edition will be out June 15, 2007. It has sold more than any other textbook in that area over the years. It's been over forty years since that book came out.

I quit my administrative job, became a professor, and ended up working my way up the ranks. I got a sabbatical leave and went to California for one year twenty-five years ago. I ended up meeting Spencer Johnson at a cocktail party. He wrote children's books—a wonderful series called *Value Tales for Kids including.* He also wrote *The Value of Courage: The Story of Jackie Robinson and The Value of Believing In Yourself: The Story Louis Pasteur.*

My wife, Margie, met him first and said, "You guys ought to write a children's book for managers because they won't read anything else." That was my introduction to Spencer. So, *The One Minute Manager* was really a kid's book for big people. That is a long way from saying that my career was well planned.

Wright

Ken, what and/or who were your early influences in the areas of business, leadership and success? In other words, who shaped you in your early years?

Blanchard

My father had a great impact on me. He was retired as an admiral in the Navy and had a wonderful philosophy. I remember when I was elected as president of the seventh grade, and I came home all pumped up. My father said, "Son, it's great that you're the president of the seventh grade, but now that you have that leadership position, don't ever use it." He said, "Great leaders are followed because people respect them and like them, not because they have power." That was a wonderful lesson for me early on. He was just a great model for me. I got a lot from him.

Then I had this wonderful opportunity in the mid 1980s to write a book with Norman Vincent Peale. He wrote *The Power of Positive Thinking.* I met him when he was eighty-six years old and we were asked to write a book on ethics together, *The Power of Ethical Management: Integrity Pays, You Don't Have to Cheat to Win.* It didn't matter what we were writing together, I learned so much from him, and he just built from the positive things I learned from my mother.

My mother said that when I was born I laughed before I cried, I danced before I walked, and I smiled before I frowned. So that, as well as Norman Vincent Peale, really impacted me as I focused on what I could do to train leaders. How do you make them positive? How do you make them realize that it's not about them, it's about who they are serving. It's not about their position, it's about what they can do to help other people win.

So, I'd say my mother and father, then Norman Vincent Peale, all had a tremendous impact on me.

Wright

I can imagine. I read a summary of your undergraduate and graduate degrees. I assumed you studied business administration, marketing management, and related courses. Instead, at Cornell you studied government and philosophy. You received your master's from Colgate in sociology and counseling and your PhD from Cornell in educational administration and leadership. Why did you choose this course of study? How has it affected your writing and consulting?

Blanchard

Well, again, it wasn't really well planned out. I originally went to Colgate to get a master's degree in Education because I was going to be a Dean of Students over men. I had been a government major, and I was a government major because it was the best department at Cornell in the Liberal Arts School. It was exciting. We would study what the people were doing at the league governments. And then, the Philosophy Department was great. I just loved the philosophical arguments. I wasn't a great student in terms of getting grades, but I'm a total learner. I would sit there and listen, and I would really soak it in.

When I went over to Colgate and got in these education courses, they were awful. They were boring. The second week, I was sitting at the bar at the Colgate Inn saying, "I can't believe I've been here two years for this." It's just the way the Lord works—sitting next to me in the bar was a young sociology professor who had just gotten his PhD at Illinois. He was staying at the Inn. I was moaning and groaning about what I was doing, and he said, "Why don't you come and major with me in sociology? It's really exciting."

"I can do that?" I asked.

He said, "Yes."

I knew they would probably let me do whatever I wanted the first week. Suddenly, I switched out of education and went with Warren Ramshaw. He had a tremendous impact on me. He retired some years ago as the leading professor at Colgate in the Arts and Sciences, and got me interested in leadership and organizations. That's why I got a master's in Sociology.

The reason I went into educational administration and leadership? It was a doctoral program I could get into because I knew the guy heading up the program. He said, "The greatest thing about Cornell is that you will be in a School of Education. It's not very big, so you don't have to take many education courses, and you can take stuff all over the place."

There was a marvelous man by the name of Don McCarty, who eventually became the Dean of the School of Education, Wisconsin. He had an impact on my life; but I was always just searching around. My mission statement is: to be a loving teacher and example of simple truths that help myself and others to awaken the presence of God in our lives. The reason I mention "God" is that I believe the biggest addiction in the world is the human ego; but I'm really into simple truth. I used to tell people I was trying to get the B.S. out of the behavioral sciences.

Wright

I can't help but think, when you mentioned your father, that he just bottomed lined it for you about leadership.

Blanchard

Yes.

Wright

A man named Paul Myers, in Texas, years and years ago when I went to a conference down there, said, "David, if you think you're a leader and you look around, and no one is following you, you're just out for a walk."

Blanchard

Well, you'd get a kick; I'm just reaching over to pick up a picture of Paul Myers on my desk. He's a good friend, and he's a part of our Center for FaithWalk Leadership where we're trying to challenge and equip people to lead like Jesus. It's non-profit. I tell people I'm not an evangelist because we've got enough trouble with the Christians we have. We don't need any more new ones. But, this is a picture of Paul on top of a mountain. Then there's another picture below that of him under the sea with stingrays. It says, "Attitude is everything. Whether you're on the top of the mountain or the bottom of the sea, true happiness is achieved by accepting God's promises, and by having a biblically positive frame of mind. Your attitude is everything." Isn't that something?

Wright

He's a fine, fine man. He helped me tremendously. In keeping with the theme of our book, *Speaking of Success,* I wanted to get a sense from you about your own success journey. Many people know you best from *The One Minute Manager* books you coauthored with Spencer Johnson. Would you consider these books as a high water mark for you, or have you defined success for yourself in different terms?

Blanchard

Well, you know, *The One Minute Manager* was an absurdly successful book, so quickly that I found I couldn't take credit for it. That was when I really got on my own spiritual journey and started to try to find out what the real meaning of life and success was.

That's been a wonderful journey for me because I think, David, the problem with most people is they think their self-worth is a function of their performance plus the opinion of others. The minute you think that is what your self-worth is, every day your self-worth is up for grabs because your performance is going to fluctuate on a day-to-day basis. People are fickle. Their opinions are going to go up and down. You need to ground your self-worth in the unconditional love that

God has ready for us, and that really grew out of the unbelievable success of *The One Minute Manager.*

When I started to realize where all that came from, that's how I got involved in this ministry that I mentioned. Paul Myers is a part of it. As I started to read the Bible, I realized that everything I've ever written about, or taught, Jesus did. You know, He did it with the twelve incompetent guys He "hired." The only guy with much education was Judas, and he was His only turnover problem.

Wright

Right.

Blanchard

It was a really interesting thing. What I see in people is not only do they think their self-worth is a function of their performance plus the opinion of others, but they measure their success on the amount of accumulation of wealth, on recognition, power, and status. I think those are nice success items. There's nothing wrong with those, as long as you don't define your life by that.

What I think you need to focus on rather than success is what Bob Buford, in his book *Halftime,* calls significance—moving from success to significance. I think the opposite of accumulation of wealth is generosity.

I wrote a book called *The Generosity Factor* with Truett Cathy, who is the founder of Chick-fil-A. He is one of the most generous men I've ever met in my life. I thought we needed to have a model of generosity. It's not only your treasure, but it's your time and talent. Truett and I added *touch* as a fourth one.

The opposite of recognition is service. I think you become an adult when you realize you're here to serve rather than to be served.

Finally, the opposite of power and status is loving relationships. Take Mother Teresa as an example; she couldn't have cared less about recognition, power, and status because she was focused on generosity, service, and loving relationships; but she got all of that earthly stuff. If you focus on the earthly, such as money, recognition, and power, you're never going to get to significance. But if you focus on significance, you'll be amazed at how much success can come your way.

Wright

I spoke with Truett Cathy recently and was impressed by what a down-to-earth, good man he seems to be. When you start talking about him closing on Sunday, all of my friends—when they found out I had talked to him—said, "Boy, he must be a great Christian man, but he's rich and all this." I told them, "Well, to put his faith into perspective, by closing on Sunday it cost him $500 million a year."

He lives his faith, doesn't he?

Blanchard

Absolutely, but he still outsells everybody else.

Wright

That's right.

Blanchard

According to their January 25, 2007, press release, Chick-fil-A is currently the nation's second-largest quick-service chicken restaurant chain in sales. Its business performance marks the thirty-ninth consecutive year the chain has enjoyed a system-wide sales gain—a streak the company has sustained since opening its first chain restaurant in 1967.

Wright

The simplest market scheme, I told him, tripped me up. I walked by his first Chick-fil-A I had ever seen, and some girl came out with chicken stuck on toothpicks and handed me one; I just grabbed it and ate it, it's history from there on.

Blanchard

Yes, I think so. It's really special. It is so important that people understand generosity, service, and loving relationships because too many people are running around like a bunch of peacocks. You even see pastors who measure their success by how many in are in their congregation; authors by how many books they have sold; businesspeople by what their profit margin is—how good sales are. The reality is that's all well and good, but I think what you need to focus on is the other. I think if business did that more and we got Wall Street off our backs with all the short-term evaluation, we'd be a lot better off.

Wright

Absolutely. There seems to be a clear theme that winds through many of your books that have to do with success in business and organizations—how people are treated by management and how they feel about their value to a company. Is this an accurate observation? If so, can you elaborate on it?

Blanchard

Yes, it's a very accurate observation. See, I think the profit is the applause you get for taking care of your customers and creating a motivating environment for your people. Very often people think that business is only about the bottom line. But no, that happens to be the result of creating raving fan customers, which I've described with Sheldon Bowles in our book, *Raving Fans*. Customers want to brag about you, if you create an environment where people can be gung-ho and committed. You've got to take care of your customers and your people, and then your cash register is going to go ka-ching, and you can make some big bucks.

Wright

I noticed that your professional title with the Ken Blanchard Companies is somewhat unique—Chairman and Chief Spiritual Officer. What does your title mean to you personally and to your company? How does it affect the books you choose to write?

Blanchard

I remember having lunch with Max DuPree one time, the legendary Chairman of Herman Miller, who wrote a wonderful book called *Leadership Is An Art*. "What's your job?" I asked him.

He said, "I basically work in the vision area."

"Well, what do you do?" I asked.

"I'm like a third grade teacher," he replied. "I say our vision and values over, and over, and over again until people get it right, right, right."

I decided from that, I was going to become the Chief Spiritual Officer, which means I would be working in the vision, values, and energy part of our business. I ended up leaving a morning message every day for everybody in our company. We have twenty-eight international offices around the world. I leave a voice mail every morning, and I do three things on that as Chief Spiritual Officer: One, people tell me who we need to pray for. Two, people tell me who we need to praise—

our unsung heroes and people like that. And then three, I leave an inspirational morning message. I really am the cheerleader—the Energizer Bunny—in our company. I'm the reminder of why we're here and what we're trying to do.

We think that our business in the Ken Blanchard Companies is to help people lead at a higher level, and to help individuals and organizations. Our mission statement is to unleash the power and potential of people and organizations for the common good. So if we are going to do that, we've really got to believe in that.

I'm working on getting more Chief Spiritual Officers around the country. I think it's a great title and we should get more of them.

Wright

So those people for whom you pray, where do you get the names?

Blanchard

The people in the company tell me who needs help, whether it's a spouse who is sick, or kids who are sick, or they are worried about something. We've got over five years of data about the power of prayer, which is pretty important.

One morning, my inspirational message was about my wife and five members of our company who walked sixty miles one weekend—twenty miles a day for three days—to raise money for breast cancer research.

It was amazing. I went down and waved them all in as they came. They had a ceremony, and they had raised 7.6 million dollars. There were over three thousand people walking, and a lot of the walkers were dressed in pink; they were cancer victors—people who had overcome it. There were even men walking with pictures of their wives who had died from breast cancer. I thought it was incredible.

There wasn't one mention about it in the major San Diego papers. I said, "Isn't that just something." We have to be an island of positive influence because all you see in the paper today is about Michael Jackson and Scott Peterson and Kobe Bryant—celebrities and their bad behavior—and here you get all these thousands of people out there walking and trying to make a difference, and nobody thinks it's news.

So every morning I pump people up about what life's about, about what's going on. That's what my Chief Spiritual Officer job is about.

Wright

I had the pleasure of reading one of your releases, *The Leadership Pill.*

Blanchard

Yes.

Wright

I must admit that my first thought was how short the book was. I wondered if I was going to get my money's worth, which by the way, I most certainly did. Many of your books are brief and based on a fictitious story. Most business books in the market today are hundreds of pages in length and are read almost like a textbook.

Will you talk a little bit about why you write these short books, and about the premise of *The Leadership Pill?*

Blanchard

I really developed my relationship with Spencer Johnson when we wrote *The One Minute Manager.* As you know, he wrote, *Who Moved My Cheese,* which was a phenomenal success. He wrote children's books, and is quite a storyteller.

Jesus taught by parables, which were short stories.

My favorite books are, *Jonathan Livingston Seagull* and *The Little Prince.*

Og Mandino, author of seventeen books, was the greatest of them all.

I started writing parables because people can get into the story and learn the contents of the story, and they don't bring their judgmental hats into reading. You write a regular book and they'll say, "Well, where did you get the research?" They get into that judgmental side. Our books get them emotionally involved and they learn.

The Leadership Pill is a fun story about a pharmaceutical company who thinks that they have discovered the secret to leadership, and they can put the ingredients in a pill. When they announce it, the country goes crazy because everybody knows we need more effective leaders. When they release it, it outsells Viagra. The founders of the company start selling off stock and they call them Pillionaires. But along comes this guy who calls himself "the effective manager," and he challenges them to a no-pill challenge. If they identify two non-performing groups, he'll take on one and let somebody on the pill take another one, and he guarantees he will out-perform that person by the end of the year. They agree, but of course they give him a drug test every week to make sure he's not sneaking pills on the side.

I wrote the book with Marc Muchnick, who is a young guy in his early thirties. We did a major study of what this interesting "Y" generation, the young people of today, want from leaders, and this is a secret blend that this effective manager uses. When you think about it, David, it is really powerful on terms of what people want from a leader.

Number one, they want integrity. A lot of people have talked about that in the past, but these young people will walk if they see people say one thing and do another. A lot of us walk to the bathroom and out into the halls to talk about it. But these people will quit. They don't want somebody to say something and not do it.

The second thing they want is a partnership relationship. They hate superior/subordinate. I mean, what awful terms those are. You know, the "head" of the department and the hired "hands"—you don't even give them a head. "What do you do? I'm in supervision. I see things a lot clearer than these stupid idiots." They want to be treated as partners; if they can get a financial partnership, great. If they can't, they really want a minimum of psychological partnership where they can bring their brains to work and make decisions.

Then finally, they want affirmation. They not only want to be caught doing things right, but they want to be affirmed for who they are. They want to be known as a person, not as a number.

So those are the three ingredients that this effective manager uses. They are wonderful values when you think about them.

Rank-order values for any organization is number one, integrity. In our company we call it ethics. It is our number one value. The number two value is partnership. In our company we call it relationships. Number three is affirmation—being affirmed as a human being. I think that ties into relationships, too. They are wonderful values that can drive behavior in a great way.

Wright

I believe most people in today's business culture would agree that success in business has everything to do with successful leadership. In *The Leadership Pill*, you present a simple but profound premise, that leadership is not something you do to people, it's something you do *with* them. At face value, that seems incredibly obvious. But you must have found in your research and observations that leaders in today's culture do not get this. Would you speak to that issue?

Blanchard

Yes. I think what often happens in this is the human ego. There are too many leaders out there who are self-serving. They're not leaders who have service in mind. They think the sheep are there for the benefit of the shepherd. All the power, money, fame, and recognition moves up the hierarchy; they forget that the real action in business is not up the hierarchy; it's in the one-to-one, moment-to-moment interactions that your front line people have with your customers. It's how the phone is answered. It's how problems are dealt with and those kinds of things. If you don't think that you're doing leadership *with* them—rather, you're doing it to them—after a while they won't take care of your customers.

I was at a store once (not Nordstrom's, where I normally would go) and I thought of something I had to share with my wife, Margie. I asked the guy behind the counter in Men's Wear, "May I use your phone?"

He said, "No!"

"You're kidding me," I said. "I can always use the phone at Nordstrom's."

"Look, buddy," he said, "they won't let *me* use the phone here. Why should I let you use the phone?"

That is an example of leadership that's done *to* employees not *with* them. People want a partnership. People want to be involved in a way that really makes a difference.

Wright

Dr. Blanchard, the time has flown by and there are so many more questions I'd like to ask you. In closing, would you mind sharing with our readers some thoughts on success? If you were mentoring a small group of men and women, and one of their central goals was to become successful, what kind of advice would you give them?

Blanchard

Well, I would first of all say, "What are you focused on?" If you are focused on success as being, as I said earlier, accumulation of money, recognition, power, or status, I think you've got the wrong target. What you need to really be focused on is how you can be generous in the use of your time and your talent and your treasure and touch. How can you serve people rather than be served? How can you develop caring, loving relationships with people? My sense is if you will focus on those things, success in the traditional sense will come to you. But if you go out and say, "Man, I'm going to make a fortune, and I'm going to do this," and have that kind of attitude, you might get some of those numbers. I think you become an adult, however, when you realize you are here to give rather than to get. You're here to serve not to be served. I would just say to people, "Life is such a very special occasion. Don't miss it by aiming at a target that bypasses other people, because we're really here to serve each other." So that's what I would share with people.

Wright

Well, what an enlightening conversation, Dr. Blanchard. I really want you to know how much I appreciate all the time you've taken with me for this interview. I know that our readers will learn from this, and I really appreciate your being with us today.

Blanchard

Well, thank you so much, David. I really enjoyed my time with you. You've asked some great questions that made me think, and I hope my answers are helpful to other people because as I say, life is a special occasion.

Wright

Today we have been talking with Dr. Ken Blanchard. He is the author of the phenomenal best selling book, *The One Minute Manager*. The fact that he's the Chief Spiritual Officer of his company should make us all think about how we are leading our companies and leading our families and leading anything, whether it is in church or civic organizations. I know I will.

Thank you so much, Dr. Blanchard, for being with us today on *Speaking of Success*.

Blanchard

Good to be with you, David.

About The Author

Few people have created more of a positive impact on the day-to-day management of people and companies than Dr. Kenneth Blanchard, who is known around the world simply as "Ken."

When Ken speaks, he speaks from the heart with warmth and humor. His unique gift is to speak to an audience and communicate with each individual as if they were alone and talking one-on-one. He is a polished storyteller with a knack for making the seemingly complex easy to understand.

Ken has been a guest on a number of national television programs, including *Good Morning America* and *The Today Show*. He has been featured in *Time, People, U.S. News & World Report*, and a host of other popular publications.

He earned his bachelor's degree in Government and Philosophy from Cornell University, his master's degree in Sociology and Counseling from Colgate University, and his PhD in educational administration and leadership from Cornell University.

Dr. Ken Blanchard
The Ken Blanchard Companies
125 State Place
Escondido, California 92029
Phone: 800.728.6000
Fax: 760.489.8407
www.kenblanchard.com

Chapter 3

DR. WILL KEIM

THE INTERVIEW

David Wright (Wright)

We are speaking today with Dr. Will Keim who has spoken internationally to over 2 million people from 2000 corporate and collegiate campuses. A Paul Harris Fellow for Rotary International, Dr. Keim's corporate clients include IBM, AT&T, Delta Air Lines, State Farm Insurance, The Ford Family Foundation, Holt International, Bushnell, Swiss Army Brands, Lenscrafters, Eye Med, Luxottica, and the Anti-Defamation League. He was awarded the prestigious Jack Anson Award by The Association of Fraternity Advisors and holds a PhD from The Oregon State University where he was voted Outstanding Professor of the Year during his graduate teaching there. He has spoken in all fifty States and most Provinces of Canada and is nationally known for excellence in public speaking and teaching. He is author of several books including *The Keys To Success In College & Life, The Truth About College: 50 Lessons For Parents Before They Start Writing Checks, Spirit Journey, The Education of Character, The Tao of Christ, Life After College,* and is a contributing author with Stephen Covey, Pat Summitt, General Alexander Haig, Jack Canfield, Nancy

Hunter Denney, and Brian Tracy in books including *Pillars of Success, Mission Possible, Let Your Leadership Speak, Lessons From The Road, and Chicken Soup For The College Soul.*

It is good to talk with you today, Dr. Keim, and that is quite a resume!

Dr. Will Keim (Keim)

Thank you, David. It is always good talking with you. The most important thing you really need to know about me, however, is that I have been married to Donna for twenty-seven years and am the father of Christa, Sami, and the twins, JJ and Hannah.

Wright

Twenty-seven years is quite an accomplishment.

Keim

Thank you, David. She continues to introduce me to people as her first husband so that keeps me on my toes.

Wright

Your children are obviously a source of great pride for you.

Keim

They have grown up with me on the road speaking and teaching. While I have been out trying to help other people's children, my wife has become in effect a single mom and I owe the lion's share of my success to her. The children (if you can call a twenty-one-year-old, a seventeen-year-old, and two thirteen-year-olds "children"), are great. They are students, student athletes, and community servants. They are all smarter than I am and I would have it no other way. Donna, however, is the glue, the heart, and soul of our family.

Wright

That is great to hear, Will. We wanted to talk with you today about our new book, *Speaking of Success,* and, as usual, you have an interesting perspective on that. Tell us what your thoughts are.

Keim

Success is a widely defined term and yet I find the words of legendary UCLA basketball coach John Wooden the most poignant. Paraphrasing the greatest coach and one of the finest Americans ever,

Coach Wooden said that success was the peace of mind that came from knowing that you did the best you were capable of doing and that you would be the only person who could ever know that. It is the internal recognition of a job or paper or presentation done to the best of one's ability. The world thrives on external evaluation, analysis, and frankly, criticism. Real success in life comes from within with the self knowledge that you laid it all on the line, left it all on the field of play, that you went "all in" in life, and therefore have peace of mind.

Wright

You have chosen to speak of success by discussing the role great speaking plays in an individual's success. Why is that?

Keim

Every great insight, discovery, or solution to a problem has to be communicated. The greatest love in the world has to enter language to be known. As a matter of fact, Dr. Martin Buber, the great Jewish existentialist and philosopher, said that the relation between person and person is unique because it enters language. He knew that human beings feel addressed by nature and by God, but the relation—the address if you will—does not enter language. Our ability to speak and our opposable thumbs have brought us upright and have given us the possibility to use language as a tool along with the things our hands can grasp.

Language is what our brains use to enter into relationships, communicate, and commiserate with one another. It is hard to believe someone could be successful to their ultimate potential without the ability so speak with words, signs, or gestures.

Wright

What are the essentials of a great speech? What does the speaker have to do to reach her or his audience?

Keim

Before I tell you, I must relate one of my most memorable experiences speaking. I was at Gallaudet University in Washington, D.C., which is a great university for the deaf. Frankly, it is plainly a great university and my audience did not hear.

I had three people taking turns interpreting in sign language for my speech because I talk so fast. In preparing for the presentation, I asked myself, "Who is a great speaker who speaks to audiences who do not or cannot know his language and is able to reach them?" The answer came immediately—Billy Graham. He speaks a sentence in English, the translator puts the sentence in the audience's native tongue, and then he picks up the sentence in the exactly the right place and with the right intonation and pitch. He is amazing, David, as a speaker and as a person.

Wright

How did you use that understanding at Gallaudet?

Keim

I would start my sentence or thought, then the signer would sign it to the audience. I would wait what I thought was an appropriate amount of time for them to decode the sign and grasp my thought or joke and then continue. When I finished, the woman who had booked me said she had never had a hearing speaker adapt his message to their audience as well as I had. And I owed it all to Billy Graham. We all need mentors like Coach Wooden and Billy Graham, even from afar, to help us actualize our gifts.

Wright

Your gift is public speaking and oratory. Share your insights with our readers.

Keim

When I speak, and every time I speak, I think of three things. I want to be:

- Precise In Detail,
- Passionate In Delivery, and
- Persuasive In Appeal.

Every public presentation should include:

- *An Introduction:* Tell Them What You Are Going To Tell Them,
- *The Body:* Tell Them, and
- *The Conclusion:* Tell Them What You Told Them.

Dr. Donald Duns shared that with me at the University of the Pacific in 1971. He was my favorite professor and a great public orator and debater. He is gone now, but not forgotten.

Wright

Break down the three major areas of the speech or presentation for us—the Introduction, the Body, and the Conclusion.

Keim

The Introduction should include:

- A *welcome and introductory comment* on the speaker's pleasure in being present,
- An *attention-getter*—An amazing fact, rhetorical question, or visual aid,
- A *credibility appeal*—Why the audience should listen to the speaker,
- A *forecast*—What is going to happen in the speech, the verbal outline,
- A sequeway/transition—"Let's move on to the topic at hand," or "Point One . . ."

The Body should include:

- *The main point(s)*—Engage the audience immediately in the topic.
- *Evidence/support*—The main point is supported by the following evidence . . .
- *Supporting/Secondary Point(s)*—Further evidence is provided by . . .
- *Evidence/expert testimony*—Utilize more evidence especially from widely accepted or known sources. For example, "On the topic of success, Stephen Covey states—"
- *Segue/transition*—This moves us in an obvious manner towards the conclusion.

The conclusion should include:

- *Refocus the assertion*—Reinforce the audience's attention on your main point(s).
- *Remind/redirect*—If you have given two sides to the argument or issue, redirect them to your point of view or assertion.
- *Call to action*—Tell them what you want them to do (i.e., no one should leave saying to themselves, "What can I do?" or "So what?").

- *Brake light*—As with a car, people like to know when you are going to stop. Say, "In conclusion . . ." or "Please, remember to . . ."
- *A parting thought and thanks*—Quotes work great here, amazing factoids, and statistics. And always thank the audience for giving you their time and attention.

Wright

You have given speeches in every state in the United States and for over twenty years. It is obvious that you think public speaking is essential to a person's success in life. Do you actually think of all these things before you speak?

Keim

Absolutely, David. My children will tell you that they often say to me, "What Dad?" And I will say, "Sorry, I was rehearsing a speech."

Everything I see in life falls into two categories for me: things that are topics for a speech or sermon, and things that need a caption such as *The Far Side* cartoon. I don't know why this is, but I can never remember a time when I did not look at the world like this. The old adage is that people do not plan to fail; rather, they fail to plan. Most great oratory looks effortless, but only because the speaker has practiced and practiced and practiced some more.

Wright

Are there any other considerations the successful speaker should consider?

Keim

Yes. Five come immediately to mind:
1. Always gather as much information about the group you are speaking to as possible.
2. Always adapt your speech to your audience and their demographics.
3. Always put yourself in the place of the listener and learner.
4. Always have fewer points and more evidence to support them.
5. Always remember it is about the audience, not you.

I have seen the "Speaking Divas" come and go—those who threw a tantrum about not having water at the podium or being picked up at the airport by a student in a small car. I have a one-page contract with no special requests. I need a podium and a microphone. I have, however, worked without either. What I need most though is an audience. Some speakers forget that and they are not successful for long, if ever.

Wright

It has been great talking with you again, Dr. Keim. Are there any special projects you are working on since we last talked?

Keim

Thanks for asking, David, and it has been good talking with you.

I am thrilled to tell you that, in cooperation with Educational Options, I have created an online course titled, "The Keys to Success in College and Life," for students and their parents who are making the transition from high school to college, and for first year college students who are already on campus. The course brings my book, *Keys to Success in College and Life,* alive with video clips. I take the students and parents deeper in the keys to success in college and life and include tips for great scholarship, the value of community service, peacemaking and conflict resolution, health and wellness issues, substance abuse resistance and education, relational tips between student and parents, character driven decision-making, and more! I am so excited about it because it is the first of many courses that Educational Options and I have planned which will include *Leadership for the 21st Century, The Truth About College: 50 Lessons For Parents Before They Start Writing Checks*, and our topic today, *Public Speaking and Success.*

Wright

How can our readers find out more about the course and how to order it?

Keim

They can log onto my Web site at willkeim.com and follow the cues. They can also check out other resources, my speaking schedule, and order my books and CDs at the store right online.

Wright

Thank you, Dr. Keim.

Keim

Please call me Will.

Wright

Thank you, Will, for talking with me today about the role public speaking plays in one's success. I wish you continued success with your teaching, speaking, writing, and new online course, but most importantly, with your family. A last thought?

Keim

Yes. Every speaker should remember that the brain can only absorb what the buttocks can tolerate. Brevity is a virtue.

Thank you, David, for giving me your time and interest. Finally, God bless you and all of our readers.

About the Author

DR. WILL KEIM has spoken personally to over two million people from two thousand collegiate and corporate campuses. His corporate clients include Luxottica, Eye Med, Lenscrafters, AT&T, IBM, The Ford Foundation, OACP, Bushnell, State Farm Insurance, and Swiss Army. He is a Paul Harris Fellow from Rotary International and holds the Jack Anson Award from the Association of Fraternity Advisors. He is the International Chaplain for Delta Upsilon Fraternity and an Intercollegiate Chaplain for The Christian Church (Disciples of Christ). Dr. Keim was selected as the Outstanding Professor at Oregon State University during his teaching there and was chosen as an Outstanding Young Man of America by the U.S. Jaycees. He is a National Collegiate Athletic Association (NCAA) recognized Speaker on Life Skills and Substance Abuse Issues, and has spoken in every state in the United States at least three times. Dr. Keim keynoted the United States Air Force Academy National Symposium on Character and Leadership with Mr. Ross Perot who said of his work, "When Dr. Keim speaks, I would advise you to listen and then live the principles he is teaching with passion and purpose." He is married and the father of four wonderful children. Dr. Keim is an avid fisherman and gardener, and the author of six books.

Will Keim, Ph.D.
Phone: 800.848.3897
E-mail: willkeim@willkeim.com
www.willkeim.com

Chapter 4

LINDA STILES

David Wright (Wright)

Linda Stiles is founder and principal of Stiles and Associates. She and her company have become an awareness catalyst for individuals and organizations seeking to ignite a positive change to achieve success. Through her personal and professional challenges she has discovered that effective change always begins within.

Her more than twenty years with three Fortune 500 oil and gas companies have been combined with an entrepreneurial spirit to build two successful businesses and model a powerful leadership message.

Linda, welcome to *Speaking of Success.*

Linda Stiles (Stiles)

Thank you, David.

Wright

Linda, you have been involved with a few projects through Insight Publishing, but why was *Speaking of Success* of particular interest to you?

Stiles

David, I enjoy sharing my core belief with the world and our cornerstone authors for *Speaking of Success* have significantly influenced that business vision. This opportunity allows me to thank Ken Blanchard, Stephen Covey, and Jack Canfield for their voices on the subject of personal empowerment, and gives me a chance to share the foundation of my personal responsibility and accountability message with my clients, my audiences, and my students.

As a professional speaker and trainer speaking on management and leadership topics, I try to use personal successes and failures to empower my audiences. I also use lessons I have learned from the self-empowerment masters to bolster my message.

There are three works from Blanchard, Covey, and Canfield that I have interconnected to add to my personal core belief.

Ken Blanchard wrote a little know book called *Whale Done!* in conjunction with Thad Lacinak, Chuck Tompkins, and Jim Ballard. This book takes the training principles used with the killer whales at Sea World and translates them into a powerful, positive message for relationships in the workplace. It exemplifies a service mindset for managers and shows the self-worth struggle we all go through when we are faced with change.

In order to change, we often need a role model and in Blanchard's book that model is called the "Training Whale." Each of us should strive to be the "Training Whale" and set the tone for positive personal and professional relationships.

Jack Canfield is known for showing the world that we are all models of success in our own unique way through his *Chicken Soup* series. It is another one of his books, *The Aladdin Factor,* that is most empowering to me. In this book he confirms that we not only need role models to follow, but we should also strive to be role models or "Training Whales" for others. To do that we must know what we want in life and go after it. After I listed 101 things I wanted in life (step three in the book) I realized I had to change my ineffective behavior so I could begin accomplishing some of those goals. Canfield teaches how to *ask* for what you want. But, before I could *ask,* I had to change some personally self-destructive habits.

In my seminars I always ask for a show of hands of those who have read Stephen Covey's, *7 Habits of Highly Effective People,* and usually about 20 percent of the group will respond. Then I ask who is actually living the "7 Habits" and only two people have ever raised their hands. Following all seven of the habits can seem daunting and I must admit that I struggle with habit number three: "Put first things first." However, the foundation of Covey's tools is action oriented personal change. The biggest change I needed to make was to stop blaming others for my problems.

It took Blanchard's positive service mentality, Covey's personal empowerment tools, and Canfield's role model pursuit to craft the personal responsibility and accountability message that is the foundation of my core belief. I would encourage everyone to read the chapters of the cornerstone authors in this book to get an in-depth look into the minds of the masters and see how each of us can achieve that feeling of personal achievement.

Wright

You have a very empowering core belief, will you tell us a little bit about it?

Stiles

My core belief states that "effective change *always* begins within." If we are not happy with the events in the life surrounding us, we have more power to change that situation than we realize. Often we become hostages to the events in our lives. We follow the same mental path as many hostages do:

- we are afraid,
- we become angry, and
- we accept our fate.

This thought process lets the events control our outcome instead of our reaction crafting the outcome. My core belief allows me to turn the mental path into a personally empowering one. It:

- stops the fear,
- transforms the anger, and
- puts you in control of your fate.

I am very fortunate to have two strong role models in my life. My parents were dynamic but very different examples of personal empowerment. I was the only child of two only children. We were not wealthy or extraordinary—just a normal family with the usual issues of the '50s, '60s, and '70s. Dad was a World War II veteran and an engineer while Mom was a housewife and mother.

My father never talked about the war but it was apparent by his appearance that he had been through a lot. He had suffered severe burns and spent four and a half years in veterans' hospitals getting skin graphs, going through reconstructive surgery, and receiving physical therapy to regain his ability to lead a normal life. The father I knew was one of quiet resolution and patience with a fair perspective on life. What a great role model for taking control of fear, rebuffing anger, and changing your view of fate.

My mother, on the other hand, is an outwardly strong person. She and I don't always agree (as with most mothers and daughters), but I had the opportunity to see her strength in action in a most enlightening way. In 1992 she suffered a stroke and spent three months in hospitals and rehab to regain her functionality. I never saw her give up or accept a doctor telling her she could not do something. Her only remaining affliction is expressive aphasia which has impaired her speech, her writing, and her reading. Watching her recovery and her resulting approach to life, she has been a phenomenal example of personal tenacity and fearlessness. What a great role model for effectively dealing with a major challenge in life.

"Effective change *always* begins within." Each of us has the power to change the outcome of the events we encounter through managing our responses. Jack Canfield aptly refers to this as his "E + R = O" formula. While his formula represents "Event + Response = Outcome," I like to translate it to "Environment + Responsibility = Opportunity." Both formulas are built on taking responsibility for your actions and being accountable for the results.

Wright

Why is being responsible for your own change, whether corporate or individual, so important to you?

Stiles

Well David, most of the world today first looks outward for causes or excuses to any personal or professional issues. Often the attitude is, "It's someone else's fault and it is their responsibility to fix it." This puts our destiny in everyone else's hands. We magically relinquish control of our lives if things aren't working out.

I honestly believe that everything happens to us for a reason—positive and negative. Some would call that predestination (our lives are planned for a specific purpose on this Earth), but I believe that we are to learn from each event, issue, or problem in order to become better models for others, not necessarily to accomplish a specific outcome.

Whether we experience issues at work, at home, with co-workers, friends, family, bosses, or children, each situation can be influenced by our response to it. In some cases, our actions may have contributed to the situation. Our actions are the only things we have to control our opportunities. It takes a lot of energy to try to change others, especially when we make no changes on our own.

Wright

How does that apply to the business environment today?

Stiles

It actually applies in three areas: management, leadership, and communication. If the message of "effective change *always* begins within" can be internalized, organizations could reduce turnover, increase employee retention, and reduce personnel cost.

According to the Society for Human Resource Management, 85 percent of those who leave a company do so because of the relationship with their manager. Now, whose fault is that? Is it the employees' for not saying anything? Could it be the managers' fault for not self-evaluating any actions taken? Possibly the organization is at fault for not training the manager how to communicate productively and effectively with employees. To stop the employee money pit, it will take the employees recognizing the need to change, managers getting out of their comfort zone, and the organization taking responsibility to invest in the skills of their leadership team so that internal changes can be effective.

There is also a generational influence to this management intolerance. Some might say the younger generations lack corporate loyalty or have a reduced pride in their work. I would also suggest that the Generation X and the Generation Y do not have the same sense of scarcity that previous generations felt about finding a job. Since their view of the job market is wide open, some will approach a management conflict by leaving the position without considering a change in themselves to keep the job. If organizations would consider changing their management image or making employee satisfaction a priority, we could then put a cap on those lost dollars. All of this comes from realizing that "effective change *always* begins within."

The second area that I mentioned was leadership. In my seminars I see so many participants who do not understand the difference between leadership and management. Leadership is the ability to empower, to trust, and to respect your employees. I do not believe that leaders are born. I do, however, think that some folks get an earlier start in practicing leadership skills. They may have a good role model—a good "Training Whale," as Blanchard would say—and realize the value of personal change as part of professional growth.

The third area of business impact for my core belief is communication. It is the foundation of both management and leadership and is very difficult to master when it comes to crisis communication. The first step in crisis communication is to control ourselves. To do that we must change our perceptions or the thoughts that support our emotions that drive our actions that ultimately have repercussions to them.

Thoughts => Emotions => Actions => Results

In order to change our result and to be accountable for our actions, we must realize that it all starts within. If we are encountering a challenging communication situation at work, we may need to change our actions, which will require a change in the underlying emotions and the governing thoughts.

Wright

What effect does your message have on your clients?

Stiles

Realizing that they have control over their business, their relationships, and their future, as well as their failures, their disappointments, and their mistakes can change a client's vision of success. We all talk about having a plan for success but what we need is a plan to learn from our mistakes. If the result of our actions/behavior/processes is not effective then we need to evaluate what contribution we made to the inefficiency and change what we have control over. This concept also applies to any effort to implement change in an organization.

If there is an initiative in place to train the leadership team, then a definitive result should be expected. A return on investment analysis should be established to discover if the change is effective. If not, then some responsibility lies with the organization to insure the expected result. Organizations often train, teach, or instruct on a critical business topic that is expected to produce strategic results, then blame the individuals when the result is not as expected. We have a tendency to put the focus on an external reason instead of looking to the internal contribution. I would have to say that most of my clients, when they take a look at our programs, often say, "We've got more control than we thought we had." Responsibility and accountability applies to corporate entities too.

Wright

This message could grow individuals within the corporate environment as well as change the business face of a company, correct?

Stiles

It is ultimately the collective actions of the individuals that will make up the image and effectiveness of an organization.

David, my offices are in Houston and I had a front row seat to watch the fall of Enron. Enron is a perfect example of where the actions of a few had a major impact on the business face of many. Ironically, the image of Enron on the street was that it was the place to be. *"You've got to work for Enron if you want to advance your career."* What an unfortunate demise. Lots of soul-searching and revision of personal plans went on that fateful day. There were some who had a hard time taking control of their lives after that and taking responsibility to change the result. This became an example of external forces that froze some individuals into inaction waiting for Enron to be accountable, which we know did not happen.

The bottom line answer to your question is *yes*. Any organization is only as strong as the individuals who lead and work there. Each individual makes a contribution. Leaders should realize that the more they build those individual contributors, the better the organization will be. Just as each individual can look internally to assess their abilities, the organization must evaluate its internal structure in order to reach their organizational goals. For them, "effective change *always* begins within" and it starts with the individual.

Wright

Why do you think it is so difficult for people to change? We all know that it is; we read it, and we hear it every day, but why do we resist accepting and acting on the need for change?

Stiles

I would have to say it's fear—fear of the unknown. We may want different results but we are not sure we can deal with changing our thoughts, our behaviors, and our actions to get those results. We are afraid of the repercussions we might suffer because we have chosen to take control of a particular result.

A second reason would be that we don't have the confidence or the tools to know what change will create the result we want. This could be a low self-esteem issue that drives the fear of the unknown result.

Wright

In sharing this message with your clients, what are your personal goals?

Stiles

My goal is to help people and organizations help themselves to rid the world of the victim mentality through fostering responsibility and accountability. Sounds rather lofty doesn't it?

Wright

A bit, but tell me how you will do that.

Stiles

I plan to chip away at this lofty goal, one seminar, one client, one presentation at a time. Each training session or presentation I do, I try to give people two things: tools and confidence. Many times the tools are not new but when presented through stories of success, as well as challenges, it becomes apparent that they can empower individuals to change the outcomes they are not pleased with. I emphasize effective action and I always define what "effective" means in terms of results.

Whether you are an employee, employer, parent, child, spouse, in-law, "out-law," neighbor, or friend, we are faced with results and outcomes every day that are both positive and negative. While the positive results of our actions fuel our motivation, the negative results defuse our effectiveness because we don't remember that "effective change *always* begins within." We have the power to turn those negative results into positive ones simply by taking responsibility for changing the way we think, which will change how we feel. How we feel will change the action we take and ultimately the results we get.

Wright

Why is this so important to you?

Stiles

I have had to recognize my personal failures, my management failures, and my business failures and realize that no one can change those results but myself. Every single day is a challenge. With every event, whether it's within the family or within the business, if I am not getting the desired result, the first place I look is internally to determine if I contributed to the result and what I can change to be more effective.

I try very hard to "walk my talk." Sometimes it is difficult, but I have to take responsibility to overcome those failures, or "ineffective results." I do this on a daily basis with even the simple things like personal communications. Practicing on the simple things helps me to perfect my approach when dealing with the major issues.

I really enjoy being the "Training Whale" for others—showing others that we can grow through our mistakes by recognizing that the opportunities in life come from taking responsibility for the environment around us. If we want to improve our life or our business we must distill the change action down to something we have control over and that would be our thoughts, feelings, and behaviors.

"Effective change *always* begins within."

Wright

Interesting. I really do appreciate the time you have spent with me today answering all these questions. I certainly have learned a lot and I'm sure our readers will.

Today we've been talking with Linda Stiles. I'm going to think about some of the things I've learned from her today.

Linda, thank you so much being with us today on *Speaking of Success.*

Stiles

Thank you, David. I have been very blessed to have this opportunity.

About the Author

LINDA STILES is best known for her enthusiasm in supporting professional and corporate change. She emphasizes that "effective change *always* begins within." She is a master facilitator and endearing presenter providing keynotes and workshops on communication, management, and leadership topics across the nation. She has twelve years of middle and upper management experience with three Fortune 500 energy companies. Linda is a professional member of the National Speakers Association and a longtime member of the American Society of Training and Development. She holds a Master of Science degree from the University of Houston.

Linda Stiles
Stiles & Associates
10878 Westheimer #290
Houston, TX 77042
Phone: 713.208.2015
E-mail: linda@lindastiles.com
www.lindastiles.com

Chapter 5

DR. JULIE SCHROEDER WALLACE

THE INTERVIEW

David Wright (Wright)

Dr. Julie Schroeder Wallace is an author, public speaker, licensed minister, life change consultant, and therapist. She earned her PhD in Counseling Psychology from the University of Oklahoma and has worked as a licensed psychologist in both inpatient treatment facilities and private practice in individual, marital, family, and group therapy.

Other work experiences include being Director of Children and Youth Ministries, Director of Family Life Ministries, Director of the Oklahoma Refugee Resettlement Program, and she served as director for numerous adult mission trips. Julie has worked in six different countries for American Conferences and Teaching Services. She has authored several series of children's and youth curriculum for churches as well as adult Bible study courses. Her most recent book is titled, *Moving Mountains One Molehill at a Time,* in which she helps people take responsibility for who they are, who they want to become, and for creating for themselves the life they want.

Her passions include growing in intimacy with God, living life to the fullest and helping others to do the same, and finding love and laughter in each day. She says her favorite titles are being a wife of twenty years to Stephen and mother of two sons, Isaiah (age eleven), and Micah (age three).

Julie, welcome to *Speaking of Success*.

What is your personal definition of success?

Julie Wallace (Wallace)

That's a great question. One of my favorite quotes is, "Everybody ends up somewhere, but few people end up somewhere on purpose." One thing that is consistent in life is change. I believe success is, in a large part, determined by our own choices about how we respond to change that is thrust upon us from outside sources and how purposeful we are in initiating changes we want for ourselves. It is easy to "go with the flow" or live the status quo. That is more of a reactive lifestyle and rarely leads to success. Being successful requires developing the qualities you want in yourself and making the choices that create a life you have chosen purposefully.

Successful people are those who thoughtfully decide where they want to end up and deliberately make the necessary changes that are most likely to take them there. Each person has to claim his or her own personal power. We all have to accept the responsibility for ourselves and become our own change agent. Purposefully choosing and changing where you are going, who you are along the way, and how you want to get there are three big keys in living a successful life.

Wright

You used the phrase, "become your own change agent." Rather than seeing change in a positive light, don't you think that most people, at least on a subconscious level, see change as a necessary evil? In fact, there have been volumes written on how and why people resist change. How do you address that issue?

Wallace

I agree that resistance to change is a common phenomenon. However, I believe that people are most resistant when they view change as something that is happening *to* them as opposed to seeing their own ability to choose it. By focusing on the inherent choices that come with any change, from the outside or within, you can better battle the resistance and are more likely to achieve the desired result. It is hard to find the motivation to successfully maneuver through changes when you fail to see the choices you are making and the impact that those choices have on your outcomes.

When given choices about what and how to change, people begin to view change in a new light. In fact, most people actually desire change. When working with a group of people I often ask a series of question such as: Would you like to see some positive change in your marriage or your relationship with your kids? Could you use an upward change for the better in your personal finances? Would you like to change even one thing about your health, fitness, or physical appearance? Are your spiritual life and your pleasure in life all you want them to be?

I have never met a person who doesn't want some kind of change in who they are, how they live, or where they are headed in life. All you have to do is look at the world around us with its 50 percent divorce rate, or the forty billion dollar a year diet industry or the statistics suggesting that the average person will change careers three to five times in his or her lifetime to know that people in general desire change.

Wright

There is a big difference between desiring a change and actually making a change. You mentioned how hard it is sometimes to find motivation. What do you believe is the best motivator?

Wallace

There is a plethora of motivations for change. Factors such as guilt, fear, shame, and competition are some of the most common causes for initiating change. I like to call these "counterfeit motivations." They may be strong enough to get you started but they rarely offer the tenacity of motivation needed to keep you going for the long haul. Proverbs 29:11 says, "Without a vision, the people perish." Most people don't end up somewhere on purpose because they don't take the time and make the effort to figure out where they want to go and intentionally set their sights on getting there. They don't have a vision. Then, rather than making deliberate and purposeful choices, they make excuses for how things didn't turn out the way they would have chosen. I'm sure you have heard the old adage, "Most people aim for nothing in particular, and usually end up achieving it." Having a clear vision gives you a measuring stick by which you can evaluate all of your choices and decisions. Developing and refining a strong personal vision of who you want to be and where you want to go in life is the best single step toward finding or creating motivation.

Wright

A clear vision is a great asset to have. How do you help people develop their personal vision?

Wallace

I like the fact that you used the word *"personal"* regarding vision. One of the first steps people often have to tackle is dealing with the visions that others have for them and how they may have adopted these by default. All too often we live out others' dreams for ourselves.

I encourage people to use a simple exercise in getting started: Pick three areas in your life in which you would like to see some change. They do not have to be the top three priorities in your life. Sometimes working on any three areas will help define what is most important to you. I suggest picking one area in which you have already successfully initiated some change but still desire more. Pick one area that is very daunting or overwhelming to face but definitely needs changing, and one that is "just because."

Write each area on the top of a piece of paper and draw a line down the middle. Use the left side to describe the way things are *now* pertaining to that area and then the right side to write down how you would like things to be. Describe in as much detail as possible both the current reality and the way you would like that area to be. It is critically important to put it down on paper. Live with it for a while and continue to add to both sides as new thoughts come to you. Don't worry about what is in between the two, just get a clear picture of where you would like to go. That picture is the vision that can keep you on track when you get to the stage of actually doing the work of making changes. Spend a lot of time imagining what your life would be like if the right side of the page were your reality.

Wright

Doing honest self-evaluation of how things currently are is hard work and so is dreaming for something bigger and better. Once a person has done all that and has it on paper, then he or she is faced with the discrepancy between the two. Sometimes that is a tough reality—to see the gap between where you really are and where you want to go. In your book, *Moving Mountains One Molehill at a Time,* you address some factors that influence a person's ability to close the gap. Will you tell us about those?

Wallace

Yes. First I caution people about becoming discouraged by the gap's size itself. The bigger the gap between where you are and where you want to go indicates the size of a vision, and a big vision can provide big motivation. Then we consider the two most important factors. The biggest factor influencing our journey between here and there is what we believe. We all have a collection of beliefs and most of us have adopted at least a few unhealthy or de-motivating beliefs. Becoming aware of and naming your beliefs can be a big help. It seems to be much easier to live out unhealthy beliefs than those that are obviously healthier.

But the good news is that you can choose for yourself what you will believe. You are the only one who gets to vote on this. I encourage people to be honest about their beliefs. They may have to look at how they live to identify them. Then I suggest that they ask themselves, "How likely is that belief, if lived out, to take me where I want to go?" If it's not too likely, then change your belief. You can choose a different belief that is more likely.

For example, if you believe that you have a slow metabolic rate and a genetic predisposition to obesity that are in control of your weight, then you are unlikely to reach a vision of losing unnecessary pounds. However, you can choose to believe that you *do* have control over your waistline and that with hard work and persistence you can achieve your goal. Obviously this belief is more helpful in making the change. So, first you have to choose healthy beliefs, and secondly you have to consistently and daily practice what you already believe.

Wright

Having a vision provides the motivation or the *Why* in making changes. But what specifics would you offer on the *How To* factor when it comes to living out healthy beliefs? Saying, "I believe something" is one thing, but practicing what I preach can be much harder.

Wallace

Living out healthy beliefs is a very tall order. I'm sure you have heard the old saying, "How do you eat an elephant? One bite at a time." If there are mountains between where you are and where you want to be, you move the mountain or move yourself to the top of the mountain by shoveling dirt one molehill at a time. I encourage people to ask themselves, "Is Today the Day?" Is Today the Day that I will make one small step, chew off one bite, or shovel one molehill that will move me in the right direction? By answering yes and taking one action, no matter how small, each day in the right direction, you will find the Yes days piling up and mountains eventually moved.

I think many of us don't make significant changes for the better because we are overwhelmed by how big the needed change is. This simple question puts the process into manageable sized bites. Maybe making it a Yes day means you put into practice what you already know or believe would be helpful, as I said earlier. Or maybe you make it a Yes day by learning more about what you want or how you can best get there. The old *Nike* commercials that used to say *Just Do It* are right. But I would say *Just Do It Today!* Say yes in some small but tangible way today toward living out healthy beliefs and moving toward your vision.

Wright

The concept sounds pretty simple. Will you give me some specific examples?

Wallace

Sure. If you want a better marriage relationship, start by making a list of all the things you *believe* contribute to a great marriage. That list might include honesty, mutual respect, support, kindness, dealing with conflict constructively, mutually satisfying sexual intimacy, quality time, forgiveness, or a willingness to seek professional help if needed. Pick one thing from that list and make today a Yes day by practicing that one healthy belief in a tangible way.

If you want to lose weight, decide today is the day that you will eat one less bite of everything on your plate or take the stairs rather than the elevator. Most people believe that the best way to lose weight is to eat less or exercise more. If your vision is to be twenty-five pounds lighter, you best move that mountain by focusing on one molehill at a time—like the plate in front of you.

Or if you want to make a career change, the first molehill might be investigating new options, exploring what training or education might be required for your new choice, or taking inventory of your own gifts, skills, and passions. Whatever the vision is, you can start moving in that direction in some small, manageable, bite-sized way today.

Making today a Yes day also helps provide extra motivation for making tomorrow a Yes day. Nothing encourages us to push on ahead more than the feeling of accomplishment or success. So, define success not as the final goal, but as having taken one step today in the right direction. You can't achieve final and big success without all the little successes along the way!

Wright

That sounds right. You have a chapter in your book titled "The Joy Factor." I love a good laugh, so this idea intrigues me. Tell us what that is all about.

Wallace

It is one of my favorite topics. I believe that laughter and joy are the best shoveling tools you can have in life! Children are born with an innate appreciation for this, but the weight of big dreams and big responsibilities can make most adults more prone to worry than laughter. The average child laughs 150 times per day while the average adult only laughs fifteen times in the same twenty-four hour period. "All work and no play make Jack a dull boy." When you continually keep your nose to the grindstone, you end up with a grossly disfigured face. Just try picturing a face with the nose all ground off—it's pretty unattractive, and life lived like that is unattractive too.

The good news is that noses can be regrown through small giggles, deep belly laughs, and truly joy-filled experiences. And having a full nose gives you a place to hang your glasses. Increasing the joy factor in your life is like putting on a pair of spectacles that help you view yourself, your relationships, your circumstances, and your goals in a more positive light. Looking through those lenses can help you see your challenges and possibilities more clearly. But I have to say that laughter and joy do not usually just happen. You have to cultivate the soil, plant the seeds, and nurture your joy crop in order for it to yield the sweetest fruits.

Wright

How do you recommend increasing one's own laugh factor or growing a personal joy crop?

Wallace

The most important key here is to be *purposeful* and to make it a priority. So often our lives are driven by attending to whatever wheel is squeaking the loudest at the moment or to putting out the biggest fire first. Cultivating laughter and joy is an area in which intentionality is usually sorely lacking.

Every day I make a "to-do" list. It always includes Bible study and prayer, laundry, taking care of my children and their needs, preparing meals, cleaning, work, and other miscellaneous duties. But I also include laughter and joy on the list. I actually write it down alongside the other priorities. Throughout the day, I check the items off as I complete them. If at the end of the day I haven't experienced a satisfactory quota of laughing and joy, then I do something about it. I pick up a funny book, tune into a funny show, I take five minutes to do something I enjoy doing, or start making plans toward something I will really enjoy in the future. It can be something as simple as taking a hot bath, eating a chocolate, having a cup of coffee outside on the back deck, calling an old friend, or working on a hobby.

Some days I have to settle for just daydreaming about my favorite activities, but I at least allow myself a few uninterrupted moments to fully enjoy the thought or memory or the dream. Most days I try to do more than just dream about it. A good place to start is to reconnect with things you once enjoyed but have let slip away and find ways to reintroduce those back into your life.

I also encourage people to be intentional about finding new possible sources of enjoyment. If you have always wanted to learn how to play the piano, do ballroom dancing, learn a foreign language, or travel, you can make today the day that you start learning, planning, or saving in some small way toward your goal. Looking forward to a big joy goal brings pleasure in the day-to-day working for it.

Wright

If you had to identify one single factor that you think contributes most significantly to a person's joy factor, what would that be?

Wallace

Generosity. Nothing will complete your joy factor more quickly or fully than giving your joy away. There are many studies providing empirical evidence to suggest that those who believe they have something worthwhile to share with others and actively do so on a regular basis receive a variety of benefits. The long list of benefits includes such things as lower blood pressure, a sense of personal well being, less illness, higher life satisfaction ratings, less depression and anxiety, and even more longevity of life itself.

Sharing your joy with others and giving your time, talents, resources, and yourself to another human being can increase your joy crop's yield exponentially. It doesn't have to be some painful or difficult sacrifice. If you love working with your hands, you can plant flowers for someone who can't. Or you might offer to do minor repairs for an elderly neighbor. If you are a real people person, you can volunteer to tutor at a local grade school or visit a nursing home. You don't have to know anyone there. In every aging facility in our country there are individuals who can use a smile, a hug, or a friendly conversation. If you love fishing, sewing, woodwork, or playing board games, there is undoubtedly a young person in your family or neighborhood or church who could use a positive role model and would enjoy sharing some time in that activity with you. Or you can help a co-worker succeed in his or her job or find a volunteer organization to join that works in an area you are passionate about.

Nothing feels better than knowing you made a difference for the better in someone else's life. Generosity in sharing your joy is, I believe, undeniably the best way to grow your own personal joy factor.

Wright

So if people want to make changes, move mountains, or increase their joy factor, what are the biggest stumbling blocks they will need to overcome?

Wallace

I like to think of stumbling blocks as cautions, like flashing yellow lights telling us we need to slow down and pay attention. I encourage people to attend to the following three Cs of caution: Craziness, Coasting, and Casting.

I define the first C, *Craziness,* as doing the same old things in the same old way, but hoping for the outcome to be somehow magically different than all the times before. If you want different results, then you have to make changes and do things differently. Stop resisting change and start purposefully choosing the changes that are most likely to get you where you want to go.

The second C is *Coasting.* Many of us get caught in the trap of just coasting through life. The problem is that you can only coast for so long or you must be going downhill. It is a simple law of gravity. Coasting and going downhill mean that you are moving farther, one inch at a time, from your mountaintop dream. Instead of coasting you can claim your own power, accept responsibility for yourself, and enjoy the privilege of creating your own life the way you want it to be.

The third C is *Casting*. Casting off what can be done today with the idea that you will do it tomorrow is dangerous. Procrastination is the direct cause of much unreached potential and many unfulfilled dreams. Believing you will change "tomorrow" is a very high-risk behavior. Tomorrow, or counting on it, is the biggest enemy of living life well today, and a life well lived today is the greatest hope of a brighter tomorrow.

The three Cs of caution are Cs for a reason. C is an average grade, and if you live with these three Cs as your pattern, you will have only an average life.

Wright

In your book you offer some remedies to overcoming the three Cs of caution. What are those?

Wallace

I call them "the three Cs of cause." If you want to live life purposefully, with a vision, it must be lived with a cause. The three Cs of cause are: Choose, Climb, and Celebrate. These may be just average Cs, but if they are lived at an A level they produce *Astounding* results.

First you intentionally *Choose* your goals. You recognize and regularly practice your power to choose for yourself where you are headed. Making choices about your life by default or not making a choice at all are both still choices in themselves and usually choices for falling or failing.

The second C is *Climb*. Stop coasting and casting and start climbing. You get your vision by choosing and you start moving by climbing the mountain one molehill at a time. You make today the day that you step out in the direction of your choosing.

The third C of cause is *Celebrate*. If you wait to get to the mountaintop before you celebrate, you are less likely to ever get there because the journey will be too hard and too long. It is important to pause for celebrations along the way! Pat yourself on the back and feel good about yourself if you made today a Yes day. Celebrate one good choice and one good action at a time, regardless of how far you still have to go. Rather than turning mountains into molehills, this is where you should turn molehills into mountains. Give yourself mountains of praise and healthy rewards for moving one molehill. This provides more motivation and energy for the molehill you will need to move tomorrow! So Choose, Climb, and Celebrate.

Wright

What is the most powerful change you have ever made and who helped you make it?

Wallace

I am constantly changing and recreating my life. Probably the biggest change for me has come in changing my vision and my beliefs. I am intentionally growing into the belief that every experience I have is a gift, and I alone can choose how I unwrap the gift within the experience and within myself. That may sound like a simple cliché but for me it has taken a lot of work and still is taking work on a daily basis. Going through major losses, disappointments, and failures, and living out the belief that there is a gift in each of those difficulties is hard. Sometimes it is even harder to live that belief in the little ongoing frustrations like traffic, broken household appliances, or interruptions.

My parents were fundamental in this process because they taught me to take responsibility for myself and to choose to be helpful to others, but not responsible for their choices in an unhealthy way. They really put me on the right path.

I have a wonderful husband who supports, encourages, and challenges me. I have a few close friends and prayer partners who hold my feet to the fire and gently push me to challenge my beliefs and live them out daily.

Just by being the people they are, my two sons inspire me to be more than I have ever been or dreamed of being.

My relationship with my Creator has to be the single most significant factor in how I view and approach change. I have been very blessed by God and I am more grateful than I could ever express in words.

Wright

If you could leave the reader with one main thought, what would it be?

Wallace

Take time to catch and grow a vision of what you want yourself and your life to be. Dream freely and dream big! Write down your dreams and your vision and keep them in front of you. Start living your dreams today by taking even one small step in the right direction. Mountains really can be moved one molehill at a time!

About the Author

DR. JULIE WALLACE is a gifted and powerful change agent whose passion is helping others become all they were created to be and live life to its fullest. She holds a PhD in Psychology and has experience as an author, newspaper columnist, private practice therapist, licensed minister, and public speaker. She uses humor, creativity, and a simple straightforward approach for turning change from a necessary evil into an adventure that is purposeful, enjoyable, and actually produces the desired results. The best one word description of Julie is "contagious"!

"I love Julie Wallace's writing style. She writes simply yet her words are profound. More importantly, she keeps me reading with her wit and sense of humor. As she makes her points, I laugh at her examples and then I think, "Wait a minute, she's talking about me!" If you've read and heard all you ever want to know about change without actually changing, I suggest you get a copy of Julie's latest book, Moving Mountains One Molehill at a Time. *I must caution you, however, this book may just change your life—for the better."*

David E. Wright, President
Insight Publishing Company

Dr. Julie Schroeder Wallace
One Molehill
E-mail: drjsw98@aol.com
E-mail: Onemolehill@aol.com

Chapter 6

JACK CANFIELD

THE INTERVIEW

David E. Wright (Wright)

Today we are talking with Jack Canfield. You probably know him as the founder and co-creator of the *New York Times* number one best-selling *Chicken Soup for the Soul* book series. As of 2006 there are sixty-five titles and eighty million copies in print in over thirty-seven languages.

Jack's background includes a BA from Harvard, a master's from the University of Massachusetts, and an Honorary Doctorate from the University of Santa Monica. He has been a high school and university teacher, a workshop facilitator, a psychotherapist, and a leading authority in the area of self-esteem and personal development.

Jack Canfield, welcome to *Speaking of Success.*

Jack Canfield (Canfield)

Thank you, David. It's great to be with you.

Wright

I talked with Mark Victor Hansen a few days ago. He gave you full credit for coming up with the idea of the *Chicken Soup* series. Obviously it's made you an internationally known personality. Other than recognition, has the series changed you personally and if so, how?

Canfield

I would say that it has and I think in a couple of ways. Number one, I read stories all day long of people who've overcome what would feel like insurmountable obstacles. For example, we just did a book *Chicken Soup for the Unsinkable Soul.* There's a story in there about a single mother with three daughters. She contracted a disease and she had to have both of her hands and both of her feet amputated. She got prosthetic devices and was able to learn how to use them. She could cook, drive the car, brush her daughters' hair, get a job, etc. I read that and I thought, "God, what would I ever have to complain and whine and moan about?"

At one level it's just given me a great sense of gratitude and appreciation for everything I have and it has made me less irritable about the little things.

I think the other thing that's happened for me personally is my sphere of influence has changed. By that I mean I was asked, for example, a couple of years ago to be the keynote speaker to the Women's Congressional Caucus. The Caucus is a group that includes all women in America who are members of Congress and who are state senators, governors, and lieutenant governors. I asked what they wanted me to talk about—what topic.

"Whatever you think we need to know to be better legislators," was the reply.

I thought, "Wow, they want me to tell them about what laws they should be making and what would make a better culture." Well, that wouldn't have happened if our books hadn't come out and I hadn't become famous. I think I get to play with people at a higher level and have more influence in the world. That's important to me because my life purpose is inspiring and empowering people to live their highest vision so the world works for everybody. I get to do that on a much bigger level than when I was just a high school teacher back in Chicago.

Wright

I think one of the powerful components of that book series is that you can read a positive story in just a few minutes and come back and revisit it. I know my daughter has three of the books and she just reads them interchangeably. Sometimes I go in her bedroom and she'll be crying and reading one of them. Other times she'll be laughing, so they really are "chicken soup for the soul," aren't they?

Canfield

They really are. In fact we have four books in the *Teenage Soul* series now and a new one coming out at the end of this year. I have a son who's eleven and he has a twelve-year-old friend who's a girl. We have a new book called *Chicken Soup for the Teenage Soul and the Tough Stuff.* It's all about dealing with parents' divorces, teachers who don't understand you, boyfriends who drink and drive, and other issues pertinent to that age group. I asked my son's friend, "Why do you like this book?" (It's our most popular book among teens right now.) She said, "You know, whenever I'm feeling down I read it and it makes me cry and I feel better. Some of the stories make me laugh and some of the stories make me feel more responsible for my life. But basically I just feel like I'm not alone."

One of the people I work with recently said that the books are like a support group between the covers of a book—you can read about other peoples' experiences and realize you're not the only one going through something.

Wright

Jack, with our *Speaking of Success* series we're trying to encourage people in our audience to be better, to live better, and be more fulfilled by reading about the experiences of our writers. Is there anyone or anything in your life that has made a difference for you and helped you to become a better person?

Canfield

Yes and we could do ten books just on that. I'm influenced by people all the time. If I were to go way back I'd have to say one of the key influences in my life was Jesse Jackson when he was still a minister in Chicago. I was teaching in an all black high school there and I went to Jesse Jackson's church with a friend one time. What happened for me was that I saw somebody with a vision. (This was before Martin Luther King was killed and Jesse was of the lieutenants in his organization.) I just saw people trying to make the world work better for a certain segment of the population. I was inspired by that kind of visionary belief that it's possible to make change.

Later on, John F. Kennedy was a hero of mine. I was very much inspired by him.

Another is a therapist by the name of Robert Resnick. He was my therapist for two years. He taught me a little formula called $E + R = O$ that stands for Events + Response = Outcome. He said, "If you don't like your outcomes quit blaming the events and start changing your responses." One of his favorite phrases was, "If the grass on the other side of the fence looks greener, start watering your own lawn more."

I think he helped me get off any kind of self-pity I might have had because I had parents who were alcoholics. It would have been very easy to blame them for problems I might have had. They weren't very successful or rich; I was surrounded by people who were and I felt like, "God, what if I'd had parents like they had? I could have been a lot better." He just got me off that whole notion and made me realize the hand you were dealt is the hand you've got to play and take responsibility for who you are and quit complaining and blaming others and get on with your life. That was a turning point for me.

I'd say the last person who really affected me big time was a guy named W. Clement Stone who was a self-made multi-millionaire in Chicago. He taught me that success is not a four-letter word—it's nothing to be ashamed of—and you ought to go for it. He said, "The best thing you can do for the poor is not be one of them." Be a model for what it is to live a successful life. So I learned from him the principles of success and that's what I've been teaching now for more than thirty years.

Wright

He was an entrepreneur in the insurance industry, wasn't he?

Canfield

He was. He had combined insurance. When I worked for him he was worth 600 million dollars and that was before the dot.com millionaires came along in Silicon Valley. He just knew more about success. He was a good friend of Napoleon Hill (author of *Think and Grow Rich)* and he was a fabulous mentor. I really learned a lot from him.

Wright

I miss some of the men I listened to when I was a young salesman coming up and he was one of them. Napoleon Hill was another one as was Dr. Peale. All of their writings made me who I am today. I'm glad I had that opportunity.

Canfield

One speaker whose name you probably will remember, Charlie "Tremendous" Jones, says, "Who we are is a result of the books we read and the people we hang out with." I think that's so true and that's why I tell people, "If you want to have high self-esteem, hang out with people who have high self-esteem. If you want to be more spiritual, hang out with spiritual people." We're always telling our children, "Don't hang out with those kids." The reason we don't want them to is because we know how influential people are with each other. I think we need to give ourselves the same advice. Who are we hanging out with? We can hang out with them in books, cassette tapes, CDs, radio shows, and in person.

Wright

One of my favorites was a fellow named Bill Gove from Florida. I talked with him about three or four years ago. He's retired now. His mind is still as quick as it ever was. I thought he was one of the greatest speakers I had ever heard.

What do you think makes up a great mentor? In other words, are there characteristics that mentors seem to have in common?

Canfield

I think there are two obvious ones. I think mentors have to have the time to do it and the willingness to do it. I also think they need to be people who are doing something you want to do. W. Clement Stone used to tell me, "If you want to be rich, hang out with rich people. Watch what they do, eat what they eat, dress the way they dress. Try it on." He wasn't suggesting that you give up your authentic self, but he was pointing out that rich people probably have habits that you don't have and you should study them.

I always ask salespeople in an organization, "Who are the top two or three in your organization?" I tell them to start taking them out to lunch and dinner and for a drink and finding out what they do. Ask them, "What's your secret?" Nine times out of ten they'll be willing to tell you.

This goes back to what we said earlier about asking. I'll go into corporations and I'll say, "Who are the top ten people?" They'll all tell me and I'll say, "Did you ever ask them what they do different than you?"

"No," they'll reply.

"Why not?"

"Well, they might not want to tell me."

"How do you know? Did you ever ask them? All they can do is say no. You'll be no worse off than you are now."

So I think with mentors you just look at people who seem to be living the life you want to live and achieving the results you want to achieve.

What we say in our book is when that you approach a mentor they're probably busy and successful and so they haven't got a lot of time. Just ask, "Can I talk to you for ten minutes every month?" If I know it's only going to be ten minutes I'll probably say yes. The neat thing is if I like you I'll always give you more than ten minutes, but that ten minutes gets you in the door.

Wright

In the future are there any more Jack Canfield books authored singularly?

Canfield

One of my books includes the formula I mentioned earlier: E + R = O. I just felt I wanted to get that out there because every time I give a speech and I talk about that the whole room gets so quiet that you could hear a pin drop—I can tell people are really getting value. Then I'm going to do a series of books on the principles of success. I've got about 150 of them that I've identified over the years. I have a book down the road I want to do that's called *No More Put-Downs,* which is a book probably aimed mostly at parents, teacher and managers. There's a culture we have now of put-down humor. Whether it's *Married With Children* or *All in the Family,* there's that characteristic of macho put-down humor. There's research now showing how bad it is for kids' self-esteem when the coaches do it so I want to get that message out there as well.

Wright

It's really not that funny, is it?

Canfield

No, we'll laugh it off because we don't want to look like we're a wimp but underneath we're hurt. The research now shows that you're better off breaking a child's bones than you are breaking their spirit. A bone will heal much more quickly than their emotional spirit will.

Wright

I remember recently reading a survey where people listed the top five people who had influenced them. I've tried it on a couple of groups at church and in other places. In my case, and in the survey, approximately three out of the top five are always teachers. I wonder if that's going to be the same in the next decade.

Canfield

I think that's probably because as children we're at our most formative years. We actually spend more time with our teachers than we do with our parents. Research shows that the average parent only interacts verbally with each of their children only about eight and a half minutes a day. Yet at school they're interacting with their teachers for anywhere from six to eight hours depending on how long the school day is, including coaches, chorus directors, etc.

I think that in almost everybody's life there's been that one teacher who loved him or her as a human being—an individual—not just one of the many students the teacher was supposed to fill full of History and English. That teacher believed in you and inspired you.

Les Brown is one of the great motivational speakers in the world. If it hadn't been for one teacher who said, "I think you can do more than be in a special ed. class. I think you're the one," he'd probably still be cutting grass in the median strip of the highways in Florida instead of being a $35,000-a-talk speaker.

Wright

I had a conversation one time with Les. He told me about this wonderful teacher who discovered Les was dyslexic. Everybody else called him dumb and this one lady just took him under her wing and had him tested. His entire life changed because of her interest in him.

Canfield

I'm on the board of advisors of the Dyslexic Awareness Resource Center here in Santa Barbara. The reason is because I taught high school with a lot of kids who were called at-risk—kids who would end up in gangs and so forth. What we found over and over was that about 78 percent of all the kids in the juvenile detention centers in Chicago were kids who had learning disabilities—primarily dyslexia—but there were others as well. They were never diagnosed and they weren't doing well in school so they'd drop out. As soon as a student drops out of school he or she becomes subject to the influence of gangs and other kinds of criminal and drug linked activities. If these kids had been diagnosed earlier we'd get rid of a large amount of the juvenile crime in America because there are a lot of really good programs that can teach dyslexics to read and excel in school.

Wright

My wife is a teacher and she brings home stories that are heartbreaking about parents not being as concerned with their children as they used to be, or at least not as helpful as they used to be. Did you find that to be a problem when you were teaching?

Canfield

It depends on what kind of district you're in. If it's a poor district the parents could be on drugs, alcoholics, and basically just not available. If you're in a really high rent district the parents not available because they're both working, coming home tired, they're jet-setters, or they're working late at the office because they're workaholics. Sometimes it just legitimately takes two paychecks to pay the rent anymore.

I find that the majority of parents care but often they don't know what to do. They don't know how to discipline their children. They don't know how to help them with their homework. They can't pass on skills that they never acquired themselves. Unfortunately, the trend tends to be like a chain letter. The people with the least amount of skills tend to have the most number of children. The other thing is that you get crack babies (infants born addicted to crack cocaine because of the mother's addiction). In Los Angeles one out of every ten babies born is a crack baby.

Wright

That's unbelievable.

Canfield

Yes and another statistic is that by the time 50 percent of the kids are twelve years old they have started experimenting with alcohol. I see a lot of that in the Bible belt. The problem is not the big city, urban designer drugs but alcoholism. Another thing you get, unfortunately, is a lot of let's call it familial violence—kids getting beat up, parents who drink and then explode—child abuse and sexual abuse. You see a lot of that.

Wright

Most people are fascinated by these television shows about being a survivor. What has been the greatest comeback that you have made from adversity in your career or in your life?

Canfield

You know it's funny, I don't think I've had a lot of major failures and setbacks where I had to start over. My life's been on an intentional curve. But I do have a lot of challenges. Mark and I are always setting goals that challenge us. We always say, "The purpose of setting a really big goal is not so that you can achieve it so much, but it's who you become in the process of achieving it." A friend of mine, Jim Rohn, says, "You want to set goals big enough so that in the process of achieving them you become someone worth being."

I think that to be a millionaire is nice but so what? People make the money and then they lose it. People get the big houses and then they burn down, or Silicon Valley goes belly up and all of a sudden they don't have a big house anymore. But who you became in the process of learning how to do that can never be taken away from you. So what we do is constantly put big challenges in front of us.

We have a book called *Chicken Soup for the Teacher's Soul.* (You'll have to make sure to get a copy for your wife.) I was a teacher and a teacher trainer for years. But because of the success of the *Chicken Soup* books I haven't been in the education world that much. I've got to go out and relearn how do I market to that world? I met with a Superintendent of Schools. I met with a guy named Jason Dorsey who's one of the number one consultants in the world in that area. I found out who has the best selling book in that area. I sat down with his wife for a day and talked about her marketing approaches.

I believe that if you face any kind of adversity, whether losing your job, your spouse dies, you get divorced, you're in an accident like Christopher Reeves and become paralyzed, or whatever, you simply do what you have to do. You find out who's already handled the problem and how did they've handled it. Then you get the support you need to get through it by their example. Whether it's a counselor in your church or you go on a retreat or you read the Bible, you do something that gives you the support you need to get to the other end.

You also have to know what the end is that you want to have. Do you want to be remarried? Do you just want to have a job and be a single mom? What is it? If you reach out and ask for support I think you'll get help. People really like to help other people. They're not always available because sometimes they're going through problems also; but there's always someone with a helping hand.

Often I think we let our pride get in the way. We let our stubbornness get in the way. We let our belief in how the world should be interfere and get in our way instead of dealing with how the world is. When we get that out of that way then we can start doing that which we need to do to get where we need to go.

Wright

If you could have a platform and tell our audience something you feel that would help or encourage them, what would you say?

Canfield

I'd say number one is to believe in yourself, believe in your dreams, and trust your feelings. I think too many people are trained wrong when they're little kids. For example, when kids are mad at their daddy they're told, "You're not mad at your Daddy."

They say, "Gee, I thought I was."

Or the kid says, "That's going to hurt," and the doctor says, "No it's not." Then they give you the shot and it hurts. They say, "See that didn't hurt, did it?" When that happened to you as a kid, you started to not trust yourself.

You may have asked your mom, "Are you upset?" and she says, "No," but she really was. So you stop learning to trust your perception.

I tell this story over and over. There are hundreds of people I've met who've come from upper class families where they make big incomes and the dad's a doctor. The kid wants to be a mechanic and work in an auto shop because that's what he loves. The family says, "That's beneath us. You can't do that." So the kid ends up being an anesthesiologist killing three people because he's not paying attention. What he really wants to do is tinker with cars. I tell people you've got to trust your own feelings, your own motivations, what turns you on, what you want to do, what makes you feel good, and quit worrying about what other people say, think, and want for you.

Decide what you want for yourself and then do what you need to do to go about getting it. It takes work.

I read a book a week minimum and at the end of the year I've read fifty-two books. We're talking about professional books—books on self-help, finances, psychology, parenting, and so forth. At the end of ten years I've read 520 books. That puts me in the top 1 percent of people knowing important information in this country. But most people are spending their time watching television.

When I went to work for W. Clement Stone, he told me, "I want you to cut out one hour a day of television."

"Okay," I said, "what do I do with it?"

"Read," he said.

He told me what kind of books to read. He said, "At the end of a year you'll have spent 365 hours reading. Divide that by a forty-hour work week and that's nine and a half weeks of education every year."

I thought, "Wow, that's two months." It was like going back to summer school.

As a result of his advice I have close to 8,000 books in my library. The reason I'm involved in this book project instead of someone else is that people like me, Jim Rohn, Les Brown, and you read a lot. We listen to tapes and we go to seminars. That's why we're the people with the information.

I always say that your raise becomes effective when you do. You'll become more effective as you gain more skills, more insight, and more knowledge.

Wright

Jack, I have watched your career for over a decade and your accomplishments are just outstanding. But your humanitarian efforts are really what impress me. I think that you're doing great things not only in California, but all over the country.

Canfield

It's true. In addition to all of the work we do, we pick one to three charities and we've given away over six million dollars in the last eight years, along with our publisher who matches every penny we give away. We've planted over a million trees in Yosemite National Park. We've bought hundreds of thousands of cataract operations in third world countries. We've contributed to the Red Cross, the Humane Society, and on it goes. It feels like a real blessing to be able to make that kind of a contribution to the world.

Wright

Today we have been talking with Jack Canfield, founder and co-creator of the *Chicken Soup for the Soul* book series. As of 2006, there are sixty-five titles and eighty million copies in print in over thirty-seven <u>languages</u>.

Canfield

The most recent book is *The Success Principles*. In it I share sixty-four principles that other people and I have utilized to achieve great levels of success.

In 2002 we published *Chicken Soup for the Soul of America*. It includes stories that grew out of 9/11 and is a real healing book for our nation. I would encourage readers to get a copy and share it with their families.

Wright

I will stand in line to get one of those. Thank you so much being with us on *Speaking of Success*.

About The Author

JACK CANFIELD is one of America's leading experts on developing self-esteem and peak performance. A dynamic and entertaining speaker, as well as a highly sought-after trainer, he has a wonderful ability to inform and inspire audiences toward developing their own human potential and personal effectiveness.

Jack Canfield is most well-known for the *Chicken Soup for the Soul* series, which he co-authored with Mark Victor Hansen, and for his audio programs about building high self-esteem. Jack is the founder of Self-Esteem Seminars, located in Santa Barbara, California, which trains entrepreneurs, educators, corporate leaders, and employees how to accelerate the achievement of their personal and professional goals. Jack is also the founder of The Foundation for Self Esteem, located in Culver City, California, which provides self-esteem resources and training to social workers, welfare recipients, and human resource professionals.

Jack graduated from Harvard in 1966, received his ME degree at the university of Massachusetts in 1973, and earned an Honorary Doctorate from the University of Santa Monica. He has been a high school and university teacher, a workshop facilitator, a psychotherapist, and a leading authority in the area of self-esteem and personal development.

As a result of his work with prisoners, welfare recipients, and inner-city youth, Jack was appointed by the state legislature to the California Task Force to Promote Self-Esteem and Personal and Social Responsibility. He also served on the board of trustees of the National Council for Self-Esteem.

Jack Canfield
Worldwide Headquarters
The Jack Canfield Companies
P.O. Box 30880
Santa Barbara, CA 93130
Phone: 805.563.2935
Fax: 805.563.2945
www.jackcanfield.com

Chapter 7

DR. ROSE GATHONI MAINA

THE INTERVIEW

David Wright (Wright)

Dr. Maina left her native Kenya at age twenty-three, nineteen years ago, in search of the American Dream. As an immigrant she had no way to work or provide for herself. She found herself homeless on the mean streets of Oakland, California. Maina didn't allow her situation to be a wall; instead, she found a way to earn her master's degree while living on the streets, using the streetlights to study. After earning her degree she went on to work with inner city kids using her example as a way to show that it can be done. She later acquired her doctoral degree from the University of Southern California (USC) in record time.

Her reputation for excellence came to the attention of the nation, resulting in Congresswoman Maxine Waters handpicking her to develop an education program and school in the worst ghetto in the country—gang-infested Watts. She escaped gun threats from the students and became affectionately known to the kids as "Mama Africa" for her ability to help people turn their lives around and achieve the American Dream. She firmly believes that the current culture and welfare of the United States is robbing many people of their birthright to live the "American Dream."

Dr. Maina's accomplishments have been featured in the *Los Angeles Times, Daily Nation, Weekly Review,* and many other local papers. The controversial Dr. Maina consistently has switchboards lit on stations where she has appeared for her no-B.S.-tell-it-like-it-is attitude. She is currently working as a certified therapist and holds a position as a college professor. She enjoys speaking to community groups about the importance of healing the inner child, removing the emotional blocks to success, reading to children, strategic planning for schools and families, and living the American Dream.

Dr. Maina's book is called: *Speaking of Success: Why foreigners are stealing the American Dream.*

Dr. Maina, is the definition of "success" the American Dream?

Dr. Rose Gathoni Maina (Maina)

I firmly believe it is. I came to this country because I wanted that American Dream. For me, if I got this American Dream I was going to be successful because the American Dream has some elements in it that I haven't found in any other place. It has got the key words of "freedom" and "love." The American Dream is, "All is possible if you're willing to work hard." It includes being free to follow your bliss and to serve others in the process.

America has been the most admired country in the world for many years for being in the position of serving the world. This is why I say that the American Dream is possible for everybody because this was what affected me when I was a young child growing up in Africa in the Gikuyu tribe—one of the largest tribes in Kenya. I really wanted this dream.

Wright

What inspired you to come to the United States?

Maina

I wanted a place where I could grow. I felt stifled in a country where I was bound and stuck in a culture where women were second-rate citizens and where what a woman could be and do was predetermined and very limited. I needed a place where people had gone to the moon. We had heard of Neil Armstrong who had gone to the moon and I said, "Wow, what a great country! I want to go there because nobody is going to stifle me. They've already been to the moon." So I really wanted to come to a place where I had an opportunity to grow, to pursue my dreams, and not be limited.

Wright

What are the four key lessons you have learned on your path to acquiring the American Dream?

Maina

The first key lesson is you must know who you are. When I first came to America it was like being in a huge candy store—there were so many opportunities. At the time I left, my country had only had one television channel. I come to America and there are over two hundred television channels! Even at the grocery store, there is not just one type of bread—there are several kinds of bread. I had difficulty having so many choices and I got lost in the maze. I desperately wanted to succeed so I determined to be whoever I could be. Soon I found myself no longer being true to who I was.

The second lesson I learned is that of entitlement. I felt that because I came from a poor country, people were obligated to help me. I quickly learned that this is a recipe for failure and if I am to succeed here in United States, then I need to expect to make the effort to do so—I am the key ingredient to my success. With this new attitude I soon embarked on the path of success.

The third lesson was to heal my life. I came in with a lot of baggage from my past and I had to use whatever means I could to find healing.

You need to heal that emotional, psychological part of you because it will slow you down and eventually override your progress and dreams. You have to let go of your past with forgiveness and gratefulness. There has been much progress made in the field of psychology—you can totally reprogram your life. You don't have to be stuck with the conditioning you received from your parents or the conditioning your society gave you. This was one of the most important lessons I learned. I had to let go of a lot of my own personal baggage and I've seen the difference. I'm moving faster toward my goals and my dreams are materializing faster.

The number four lesson I learned was the fulfillment that came from making a contribution—of doing what I love and doing it so well that I could be of service to others.

I think that is so important. America has the highest number of volunteers in the world. American people have gone all over the world volunteering their services and giving aid. The value of contribution is very much ingrained in the American culture.

Wright

What obstacles did you have to overcome?

Maina

I got here without a plan. For eight years I was so focused when I was in Kenya on saving to come to America that I hadn't really thought out a plan of how to stay in the United States. That resulted in my being homeless for two years living on the streets and moving twenty-two times. However, in the process I did earn my master's degree.

The other problem I faced was that I had no immigration papers that would enable me to work here. Being a visitor, I wasn't allowed to work so I had to take menial jobs even though I was over-qualified for them. I would barter my services to clean people's houses and take care of their children so I could have room and board.

Another obstacle I had to overcome was being "black." I never was considered black in my country. I am Kenyan and from the Gikuyu tribal community. When I came here people told me I was black, but I'm a brown-skinned woman. I kept telling them, "I'm brown, I'm not black. What are you talking about?" For five years I continued telling people that I'm Kenyan, I am brown, and that I didn't know what they were talking about. I couldn't understand why they were pigeonholing me in that way. I had just come here thinking that I was just a person and that I was free. I didn't understand the racial issue. For the first time I had to embrace the fact that I was black and there was a certain way that black people are perceived. I soon learned what I could say and what I should never say—how to be "politically correct."

Wright

What are your thoughts on stereotypes?

Maina

Most people do not understand how much stereotyping hinders success. One thing I tell my students is that you've got to roll up your sleeves and work. You shouldn't claim entitlement because you're black or from a minority group. You get in there and work for it.

Yet even as I say this I am reminded of an incident that hurt me deeply. I had gone to a fair and was among a huge crowd of people watching the very clever police dogs do tricks. I asked the officer in charge what one should do if a fierce dog came charging at them. He said, "Just don't steal anything." I walked away feeling humiliated. Two women followed me and apologized for the police officer's rudeness saying it was uncalled for.

I didn't get over this hurtful incident for almost a year. I finally shared it with a real estate agent who filed a complaint to the chief of police. I received a call from the chief who apologized and let me know that the police officer had been reprimanded.

Wright

In your opinion, does the glass ceiling still exist for women and if so, how did you break through it?

Maina

In my opinion it still does exist. I hear many corporate women in America complaining that they don't get the same privileges as the men. The women are just as qualified and sometimes the men are less qualified than the women are.

I've worked with a few of them and I've asked them what it is that's limiting them. I've asked, "Is it within you or do you think it's coming from somewhere out there that you can't control?" A lot of them tell me that there is a glass ceiling.

Here I am, having left my country and having had enough of being treated like a woman who can't do this and can't do that. I come to America where there is much more going for women and I find that gender is still an issue.

I have worked in the female dominated field of Early Childhood Education for years. Now I'm working at colleges and universities; this is where I'm bumping against that glass ceiling a little bit more.

Healing the past, the little girl (inner child) has been very effective in helping me and other female clients break through the glass ceiling. One professional woman—a client of mine—has a better relationship with the men at her workplace because through therapy we were able to heal the inner child in her who grew up ignored and unheard by her father.

Wright

Does racism still limit the success of individuals?

Maina

Yes, unfortunately it does. I've been in America now for eighteen years and still to this day people will treat me differently. I'm sounding more American but my accent is still there. I continue to work on speaking the way Americans speak; I just need to get in the rhythm. I will speak for a while and then I'll slip back into my accent.

Racism does exist in the sense that people treat me differently until they get to know me. When first meeting someone, there will always be that initial span of time when you are first getting to know one another. It's as though you have to prove yourself because of this unspoken barrier.

I have told my inner city students that as long as they do what they need to do with integrity and they have the courage to be who they are, it doesn't matter what people think because their hard work will pay off in the long run.

America is still a country that honors hard work. One of my clients said to me that it is who you know that counts and my swift reply to him was that I had met people with all the right connections but no hard work and proof of experience to get a job well done.

Wright

How does being from another place, in your case Kenya, help you in acquiring the American Dream?

Maina

As an outsider you can really see a country with a fresh set of eyes, whereas the people who live there take a lot of things for granted. I can't afford to take America for granted because I know where I came from. I have a choice between where I came from and making a new life for myself here. That ability to choose gives me a huge advantage.

I hear people complain about politics in America. I have another reference of politics. In Kenya, politics is very corrupt because there is no control—there is no system of checks and balances. In America there is a system where the three major parts of the government—legislative, executive, and judicial—limit the power of each other.

The freedom and opportunity in United States cause me to work harder and take advantage of opportunities that come my way, no matter how small they are. People wonder why I would work in a job that pays less than another. For example, when I took the job in the inner city, a lot of my black friends said they would never go there.

They said it wasn't the kind of place for them and it was certainly not the kind of place for me. But I said it was a starting point and because I took that job it catapulted my career in so many ways; even to this day I am still benefiting. You have to start somewhere, no matter how small it is.

I have clients who come from other countries like Mexico and El Salvador who are willing to take a menial job. They look at the menial job as a stepping stone—a beginning. There are people who are sitting at home right now who are natural born citizens of the United States and who will not work for five dollars an hour because they believe the job is beneath them. They prefer to get a welfare check.

Coming from another country, I have a different perspective. The eyes of an outsider are a true gift. I teach people how to become outsiders within their own country. I think this is a gift you can give anyone who's American. People come to my workshops to be able to pull themselves out of their complacency for awhile. Through the techniques I have developed they are able to gain a new perspective. It is wonderful to hear them say, "Oh my God, thank you for helping me value my country, the United States of America!"

Wright

What are the seven key steps anyone can take to achieve the American Dream?

Maina

These are very simple. The first step is you must decide what it is that you want to do. Decision-making is very important. I find a lot of people are very indecisive—they don't know what they want. You really have to find what it is that motivates you. Is it money that motivates you? Is it death that motivates you? For me, for a long time it was death that motivated me. I would think, "Oh, I must do this before I die."

The second step is being committed. You must make a "live or die" kind of commitment. Napoleon Hill, who wrote the book *Think and Grow Rich,* speaks of a great warrior who would burn his ships when landing in a territory he wanted to conquer. He would tell his men, "Listen men, we will either win or perish!" It's important to have that kind of commitment where there is no retreat.

When I left Kenya to come to the United States, I "burnt my ship." I just said, "There is no coming back, forget about it." I canceled my job and said goodbye; that was it. I refused to take anybody's money to come to America because I didn't want to owe anyone anything. It took eight years to save for a plane ticket but because I burned my ship I was committed to succeeding.

The third step is to organize. You must have a blueprint. You must be able to think through as much as you can about what it is that you want to accomplish. This is critical step because without a plan you are not going anywhere.

The fourth step is to visualize—you must declare your dream. Know what it is you're going for. I love closing my eyes before I go to sleep and picture my dream and its end result. Then I live there for a few minutes.

When I was making my plans to come to America my entire bedroom was filled with memorabilia of America. I had an American flag and a map of the United States with each state and every city on it. My suitcase was packed, I was ready to go. Before I went to bed I would trace with my finger going from town to town, city to city. For eight years I traced along that map with my little finger. I had very little money; but I saved a dollar every month during the last few years before I came. I know that it's possible to get through by just wanting something so badly. I don't know how it comes together but it does.

Along with visualizing, you must declare your dream. Declaring your dream is like a being wrestler. Wrestlers walk around the ring making bold statements like, "I'm better than Stone Cold Steve Austin and tonight I, the Undertaker, will tear him in pieces!"

I wanted my doctorate so badly and I wasn't getting it as fast as I desired, so I started calling myself Dr. Maina six months before I actually received my degree. I said, "Hello, my name is Dr. Maina," to myself and when I presented workshops I wrote that Dr Maina is the presenter. I began to declare who I was and believe me, as soon as the flyers were out with my name on them as Dr. Maina, I knew that I'd better be Dr. Maina by the time I arrived at that workshop. So I did my entire dissertation from approval to completion in three and a half months! Visualization and declaring are both very important elements of realizing your dream.

The fifth step is consistency. My friend, you will never get anywhere unless you're taking consistent, persistent action. Do something every day that moves your dream closer to fulfillment. There is no such thing as something for nothing. As an education consultant I visited many institutions and saw many employees being slothful at work. They complained about their wages and neglected to realize they were violating the immutable law that you do reap what you sow.

The sixth step is my favorite, which is to reinvent. You must re-adjust, rework, and fine-tune your dream. Many times I've set out to accomplish a dream only to find out that it was not what I wanted, however, I found the true hidden dream in the process. Had I neglected readjusting and reworking that first dream I would have never found the second dream—the dream I really wanted. In 1998, I set out to become a superintendent of schools and found my true dream of being a college professor; I love teaching.

The seventh and last step is you must rehearse. Rehearse your victory and success over and over. Rehearsing your dream means you go over it and over it. You do this as many times as you can every week so that you really know it. It is just like rehearsing for a performance, you need to rehearse dreams too.

As an actress our troupe rehearsed performances in Kenya two months prior to presenting a show. That was very helpful because we knew the acts inside out. When we finally opened the show, our performance was superb. That's why I say rehearse so that your dreams will be superb and you will present a stellar performance. So I rehearsed my dreams a lot.

These are the seven critical steps that I can think of right now to help people achieve their American dream.

Wright

What would you advise parents and educators to do to prepare young children and youth for success?

Maina

It's very, very important to listen to what children and young people are telling you. And it's very important to observe what they love to do and what excites them. I find that teachers and parents often have their own agenda and what they want for their child. They totally miss the point. The point is, it's not about them—it's about the children.

You must be able to listen to your children, to observe what they like, and help them grow their dreams. Help them develop a plan to get what they want. Everybody comes into this world able to do something and the best gift you can give people (and this is why I believe so much in the work I do) is to enable them to get that which they came to do. That is the role of being a parent. That is the role of being a teacher. These are two very key jobs in any nation—being a parent or being a teacher.

To me these are two critical roles that any nation needs to honor and to elevate. It is important to pay these people well and provide them with the resources they need to do these jobs well because young people are the future of any nation. Any nation that ignores children and young people is definitely a nation that is going to be in danger. I advise parents and teachers to care for children well because they are our future leaders. They are the ones who will take care of us when we grow old. In America we need to do a better job of taking care of our young people. We need to listen, observe, and help children find out what makes them excited inside.

I had one student in my classroom who didn't know what she wanted to do in life. I asked her, "What would you do if your life were going to end in six months or one year? What do you really want to accomplish before you die?" Another favorite question is, "If I gave you one million dollars in cash, what would you want to do? Would you want to be here in the classroom with me learning about teaching young children?" "Hell no!" she said. She wanted to be a pilot and fly planes. I told her she'd best get out of my classroom and get on with it. I told her to go repair planes for a while. I told her to learn all about flying them—there were places that would even pay her to do this. She went and did that for a year. She came back and told me that she'd changed her mind—she just wanted to work with children. But at least she went and tried it. She still thanks me to this day by referring many students to take my classes.

Wright

Your life's work and mission has a theme of the power of service and the greater good for all. How does this manifest in individual success?

Maina

This is a tough question because when a lot of people think of being successful and reaching their dream, it's all about them. For me, at one time it was all about me for awhile. I was going after my dreams and I kept thinking only about what would happen to me. But as you go along and you start fulfilling dreams at the speed I am, you begin to realize, "Gee, this is not fulfilling."

I was able to get a brand new car—the car of my dreams. I had wanted this car for ten years and I drive it now with the top down.

It's a beautiful sports car, made by a top-of-the-line auto manufacturer and I just love my car. It fulfills me to a certain extent but it doesn't fulfill my need for doing something for the greater good of all. I had focused just on the material side of success.

Then I began to revamp some of my dreams to include my desire for doing something for the greater good of all and I found a deeper sense of fulfillment. It's great to drive the car of my dreams but it doesn't give me that sense of fulfillment. People like Mother Teresa have a bigger dream than just satisfying their own desires; other people are included in it. When I began to study the lives of great contributors to human welfare I began to realize that this was the missing element for me and that I wanted it. It's part of the reason why I stay teaching in the inner city. I get a sense of fulfillment in giving back and empowering people who really need to just get out from where they are and see life in another way—leaving a life of entitlement for a life of contribution and the greater good of all.

I urge my clients to make sure that they have those kinds of dreams because they're going to find out that when they are very successful they will want and need more. I really believe that people who have altruistic, higher dreams will end up making valuable contributions.

Bill Gates is another person who has higher dreams. He is giving away a lot of money to charities; he is contributing to the greater good of all.

However, another important point to make is that you will never be able to give anything until you've given something to yourself. For me the car of my dreams helped me realize my next dream of living in one of the best neighborhoods in the country. I am someone who lived on the streets, homeless and, like Scarlett O'Hara of *Gone with the Wind* who swore she will never go hungry again, I vowed never to be homeless again and to one day live in Beverly Hills, California. And that's where I currently live.

Wright

You are an accomplished visual and performing artist. How has creativity aided you in accomplishing so many of your dreams in record time?

Maina

The one thing that I can say is that being a visual and performing artist forces you to be creative. When you tap into your creative intuition and you have an imagination, it is a gift. Creativity will help you see your dream; you will be able to see every step and the end result.

Sometimes I don't see every step so I role play as an actress or I paint it as a visual artist. I put it out there so that it can speak to my soul and I can tap into it anytime. In my living room, I act out how I want my dream to be and tell the story of how I achieved my dream. Some people use affirmations but I find the retelling, role playing, and creating a vision board (which I do by painting) to be very powerful because my subconscious is being imbued with my dream.

Creativity will enable you to get your dream out of your head into the realization of it. You begin to take notice of opportunities you have not noticed before. Your subconscious is already in the process of getting that dream because you've empowered it through creativity and imagination. This is very important when you're going after a dream.

Wright

You have accomplished a great deal. What is your key secret on time management?

Maina

Oh, you can't control time. People want to have more hours in their day but everybody has the same amount of time. That's the saddest thing I found out. However, it's all about how the time you have is spent that determines whether you're going to be a successful person on a consistent basis or if you just waste time.

There are many distractions that steal time. The biggest thief of time is television. There are many people watching television who will tell you they are watching the news and other important shows. I say, "No you're not!" There are different ways to get the news. People are always going to talk about important news events. I've had no television for the past six years—absolutely no television. This has enabled me to change my life rapidly. I was able to move in to my dream neighborhood, Beverly Hills, because of reading real estate and business books that taught me how to recognize and close a great deal.

Listening to tapes in my car driving to work instead of listening to the radio was also helpful. Los Angeles traffic is atrocious, so I had a lot of time to listen to tapes; my car is my university. My home is a place of learning. There are books I've read seven times just to live out in my life the ideas they teach. I advise my clients and students to read every day for thirty minutes. I started out with ten minutes a day then went up to thirty minutes. Now I read for one hour and a half every day before I sleep.

Another thief of time is personal calls. I have told my friends that I am unavailable during my prime time. Prime time is when I'm most creative, when my whole body is alert. I don't like to just chat on the phone. I prefer to talk business or talk about something helpful. What is it that you want? Do you want friends who contribute to your learning something or do you want friends who just waste your time? I have had many mentors. They all say that the friends I associate with determine the level of success I will reach. If those friends are not raising their level of self-development and improving their own lives going after what they want, then they will eventually pull me down. I began to take a hard look at my circle of friends. I'm afraid to say I had to let some of them go. I realized some of them were depriving me of energy I needed for myself.

Now I have friends I can have a business meeting with, but we can meet more casually when it's appropriate. These friends help me keep my focus on what it is I want to accomplish and how I can in turn be of benefit to them. What you want and what kind of friends you have are important questions to ask yourself, otherwise you're wasting your time. Your time is gone—you never recuperate time that is wasted. Two time stealers for me were people who did not understand the value of time and television. Television is interesting but I have no time to watch other people getting their dreams—I've got to go and get mine.

About the Author

DR. ROSE GATHONI MAINA left her native Kenya at age twenty-three, nineteen years ago, in search of the American Dream. As an immigrant she had no way to work or provide for herself. She found herself homeless on the mean streets of Oakland, California. Maina didn't allow her situation to be a wall; instead, she found a way to earn her master's degree while living on the streets, using the streetlights to study. After earning her degree she went on to work with inner city kids using her example as a way to show that it can be done. She later acquired her doctoral degree from the University of Southern California (USC) in record time.

Her reputation for excellence came to the attention of the nation, resulting in Congresswoman Maxine Waters handpicking her to develop an education program and school in the worst ghetto in the country—gang-infested Watts. She escaped gun threats from the students and became affectionately known to the kids as "Mama Africa" for her ability to help people turn their lives around and achieve the American Dream. She firmly believes that the current culture and welfare of the United States is robbing many people of their birthright to live the "American Dream."

Dr. Maina's accomplishments have been featured in the *Los Angeles Times, Daily Nation, Weekly Review,* and many other local papers. The controversial Dr. Maina consistently has switchboards lit on stations where she has appeared for her no-B.S.-tell-it-like-it-is attitude. She is currently working as a certified therapist and holds a position as a college professor. She enjoys speaking to community groups about the importance of healing the inner child, removing the emotional blocks to success, reading to children, strategic planning for schools and families, and living the American Dream.

Dr. Maina's book is called: *Speaking of Success: Why foreigners are stealing the American Dream.*

Dr. Rose Gathoni Maina
E-mail: drgmaina@yahoo.com

Chapter 8

ANNETTE FAZIO

THE INTERVIEW

David Wright (Wright)

Annette's twenty-five years of leadership experience has made her uniquely qualified to teach, inspire, train, and motivate people at every level of business.

Annette started her business, Fazio's Italian Restaurant and LaStalla Pizzerias, in 1986 in Southern Maine and managed a staff of more than eighty. Annette developed and marketed her own line of specialty foods, was a project manager and host for a Boston cable television cooking show, and was a continuing education instructor for Le Cordon Blue.

Annette's infectious, quick-witted humor, creativity, and personality complement her professionalism to produce effective and entertaining seminars, presentations, programs, and meetings that you and your employees will find both enjoyable and useful.

Annette, what was the biggest obstacle to overcome on your journey?

Annette Fazio (Fazio)

I would definitely say it was the feeling of being *less than* just about everybody around me—I believed that most people knew more than I did or were more capable and could do it better.

Wright

In the restaurant business you mean?

Fazio

No, it wasn't confined to the restaurant world it was just about in all the areas of my life. I think it had a lot to do with my upbringing. Things were different in the fifties and my family struggled financially, not that we were different from my neighbors—the neighborhood was just a tad on the "wrong side of the tracks."

A college education wasn't considered because it was out of the financial realm and on top of that I always felt like I was out of the loop in school—out of the achievers' circle, so to speak. It was not because I wasn't smart, but because I was always going against the tide by seeing things differently. I didn't fit into the box. It didn't seem to be a big deal because the family belief was I would get married and raise a family anyway and my school life was not that critical.

What I realize now is my slightly off-the-wall, entrepreneurial spirit was budding and I had a different view of life than my classmates. I just didn't quite fit into the mold and I was usually vocal about it. I spent some serious time visiting with the principal—it's good to make friends in high places.

Wright

What possessed you to change your lifestyle and start up your own business, especially the all-consuming business of restaurants and food service?

Fazio

First and foremost I would say insanity; a little insanity is always helpful when you are taking that big of a risk. Food is one of those things that sincerely gives people joy and I knew my way around the kitchen. I wanted to contribute in a way that would make a difference and food was a logical path. It started in 1982 when I spent four months in Washington, D.C., as a volunteer at the Women's Movement headquarters.

I left Washington with two messages: 1) accomplishment was possible if you believed, and 2) a better understanding of women's struggle to succeed.

Achieving greatness in the business world was not something I dreamed about. Becoming a business owner wasn't in my master plan, even though I knew I was smart enough to make something happen if that was my choice. The universe didn't quite agree with my plan of settling down and skipping the business world altogether.

I had no interest in the business world because I always felt out of place and I didn't take direction well. I had a number of jobs out of high school all working for large traditional companies like the New York Telephone Company. The telephone company was my first full-time job and in 1965 it was the only telephone company in America. It was a typical big company with big company mentality, rules and regulations, a supervisor, twenty women in a unit, and me.

It never occurred to me how difficult I was until many years later when I was visiting a store in Long Island. There was instant recognition with a woman I came face-to-face with. Have you ever had that feeling when you encounter someone and you both realize you know each other but you don't have a clue from where? We ran down the usual possibilities but it was not the same neighborhood, church, schools, or bars. It hit us at the same time—work. We both had worked at the New York Telephone Company. Her eyes got big and wide. She pointed at me and blurted out, "I remember you; you never thought the rules applied to you!"

I don't know about how you would take that kind of comment, but I didn't take it as a good sign that this was the first thing she remembered about me. I knew in my heart it was the truth but I could not zero in on what she was referring to.

She recognized the "deer in the headlights" look on my face and went on to say she was the union rep and we were always in the supervisor's office trying to save my job. Ah, it all came flooding back to me; but being older and wiser I immediately felt an instant pang of guilt. Obviously I wasn't among her fondest memories.

"This should make you feel better," I said. "I have eighty employees now and about 60 percent of them don't think the rules apply to them either."

Her eyes got bright and immediately a look of satisfaction came across her face. She smiled and said, "It was nice seeing you," and walked away, perfectly content that the stars had finally aligned and justice had been served.

The fact that I never thought the rules applied to me was exactly the belief that enabled me to succeed against the odds. There is a 90 percent failure rate in the restaurant business and I broke all the rules going in. I was not a trained chef, I had no business experience, I had never worked in a restaurant of any kind, and when I started the process I had no idea how the food was prepared so quickly and sent out of the kitchen.

As an employee, if I saw something that had to be done I did it, whether it was my job or not. I was once told not to answer the phone because it wasn't my job. True story: the receptionist stepped out and her phone rang and no one was answering it or planning to. By the fourth ring I answered it. I handled the call properly but I was reprimanded because answering phones was not in my job description. I had direct orders to let it ring next time. I didn't (voice mail had not been invented yet). My behavior was considered disruptive to my supervisor and not answering the phone was just bad business in my opinion. In case you haven't figured it out, I was a supervisor's nightmare.

My time in Washington D.C., had an effect on me. I began to have this nagging feeling that I wanted to create and achieve something. I chose something I was most comfortable with: people, food, and cooking. I became a consumer advisor for Cuisinart Food Processors. I conducted cooking classes that incorporated techniques and training on the proper use of the food processor. I would also travel to different stores in the New England area educating store managers and sales associates on the mechanics and benefits of the product and why every cook should have one.

I also started a small specialty food business delivering to local businesses. The product was very popular but I wasn't sure I wanted to be in the food manufacturing business so I kept the business small.

My friends had this bright idea that I should start a restaurant. Why not? I could cook and people liked my food. I personally didn't think it was that great of an idea, but they nudged and supported me and I warmed up to the concept. I opened my first restaurant in 1986 and eventually I opened three restaurants.

I look back now and realize that this was an exceptional feat considering my total lack of experience (Note: starting a business that way is not widely recommended and the bankers practically fall off their chairs laughing when you ask for money.)

Wright

Was there one person you admired who gave you the courage to never give up?

Fazio

There were two men in my life: one was my father and the other is my brother, John.

My dad was born in 1896 and was a young father through the depression who experienced some very hard times. He found his strength through the love he had for my mother. My dad respected his wife and adored his family. He never let go of his dreams. As long as he had a breath in him he had dreams and he believed in possibilities. He would see a location and comment on it being a perfect spot for some particular kind of business. Eventually someone would come along and open the same business in that same spot and the business would succeed. He was a visionary with no cash. Unfortunately, when he did take a leap, his vision didn't work for his own ideas. My dad started a number of businesses between 1920 and 1946 and became part of the statistic of 80 percent of all new businesses that fail. My father died at age sixty.

My brother, John, is twelve years older than I and although my father never realized his own dreams, my brother was paying attention while Dad was dreaming. John took some of my father's ideas and turned them into successes. There are a couple of risk-takers in the family.

My paternal great-grandfather started a macaroni and bread factory in Sicily. My paternal grandfather came to America in 1908, landed in New York City, and soon after started a pasta and bread factory in Scranton, Pennsylvania. At twelve years old my father was traveling between Scranton and New York City for supplies in a horse and wagon (a solid four-hour drive today). You might say I come from sturdy Italian stock.

In Scranton, the factory and home was sabotaged and was burned out of business because my grandfather refused to pay protection money to organized crime. They blew up his home and tried to kill his entire family (talk about pushy and rude). The story goes that my grandmother woke up with a terrible premonition and made the family leave the house seconds before it blew up. It broke my grandfather's spirit but my dad still believed in the American dream.

When my father died, my brother—the third of six children—became the patriarch of the family. He's a strong individual, mentally and physically. As a young man he was first mate on a tugboat on the New York waterways and then he became a New York City Fire Fighter. Through the years I watched him take risks, both financially and physically. Sometimes he came out on top and sometimes he didn't—both physically and financially.

I saw courage in motion in both my father and my brother. I learned firsthand that risk is part of the process.

Wright

What was your diving force?

Fazio

People and service to others as well as myself. I didn't always recognize the service part of my life but looking back over the years, it was always about people. Today it's important that I check in with myself on how I'm serving others around me and if I am a contributing factor to my own life and enriching the lives around me.

When I started my business I wanted something more. I wanted to feel more passion in my life regarding my family and my community. I wanted to feel a sense of accomplishment and I wanted to experience belief and pride in myself. I needed to do something that I could point to and be proud of for myself and my family.

Wright

Sounds to me like you're endorsing responsibility.

Fazio

That is exactly right. Our lives are our own responsibility; we are contributors to the outcomes. I wanted to be the best at what I was doing for my own satisfaction and I wanted others to benefit. I took a look at my life and realized that good values kept me strong and faith held me up when life became difficult.

When I thought things looked a little bleak I looked for opportunities to be of service; my business helped me bring that goal to a new level. I tapped into a lot of avenues that I could give to the community—to people who needed a little help.

I investigated organizations to see how they would fit my need for contributing. There are two organizations that have given me as much as I've given to them. One is Rotary International. Rotary was a major source of gratification and service and so was the youth ministry in my church. I had the opportunity to be an adult leader for the youth mission trips with the teenagers of my church. They traveled to different parts of the country and what I have received in return is priceless. How it felt to see those teenagers growing in love for their fellow members in the community of life was wonderful. (That is, right after my nervous system got over the shock of having forty teenagers with me twenty-four hours a day for several days!) Watching these kids helping people who can't help themselves, such as the aged, the infirm, or young families who are working as hard as they can and need a helping hand, is an incredible experience.

In the everyday grind I can sometimes forget how precious and short life can be. I wanted to bring that joy into my family's life. If that is my goal, whose responsibility does that become? I learned a long time ago that we are responsible for our lives and it's important to be pro-active in the outcome.

I know I haven't mentioned money yet. Don't get me wrong, I like money—it is right up there with oxygen; but I also believe if money is your driving force, then where does the joy come from when something happens to the money? What happens if you lose the money? What's left? Money is a great medium but it can only be part of the equation.

So my driving force has always been something that no one can take away from me, through the fair weather and through the storms. There will always be people to connect with and it's my responsibility to connect with them.

Wright

From your point of view what does success look like?

Fazio

Success is being respected and having the love of people you are in community with, not just family but the community of all the folks I interact with. My aim was to love and raise independent children and integrate my business with my family values, bringing pride to my family while creating a bond with the community. The same criteria holds true for my speaking career. I feel a sense of pride about the work I do and how I feel about me. At the end of the day it's only me in the mirror. Stephen Covey talks about making those daily deposits in the emotional savings account. Building that account is important, especially on the rainy days and we all have them.

It is not only the big things, it's the little things too. I was asked to judge a gingerbread house contest and out of the forty-seven entries, thirty-six of them were families with children under the age of eleven. Being included in that is an example of one of the small joys that I get in return.

I also think it's important to know the difference between serving your community and not being able to say no. Discernment and being adept in defining the two is a huge part of success. The eighty/twenty rule is always in play and sometimes we need to ask ourselves if we are just picking up the slack or are we contributing to the community because we want to.

Success is also enjoying your success—sitting back on occasion and appreciating what you have and how you got there.

Wright

What two or three things do you attribute to successful practices in business and life?

Fazio

Seeking advice and asking for input from people I admire and respect. Another would be to believe in yourself. The third is to always look to the future with a positive attitude—believe in the possibilities.

For example, I knew I didn't have all the answers, nor would I ever. I look at my success like the turtle sitting up on the fence—he didn't get there alone. Sometimes our minds convince us we should know the answers but the mind can be a tricky thing. A friend of mine said that the mind is a dangerous neighborhood—don't go there alone. Left to its own devices the mind will diagnose illnesses with no medical training, it will project a financial future (usually bleak) with nothing to substantiate it, and it can put an unbelievable fright into us with no hard evidence of real threat.

If you are at all unsure, it's always best to run it by someone else. But be cautious; don't ask just anyone standing close to you—go to the people who understand where you're going and get feedback from them. There is a huge difference between seeking advice and living by somebody else's plan. You have to separate the two. Make the decision to listen without interrupting and decide what information is useful to you and what is not. Some advice is good; some advice is great, but if it won't fit with your personality it's useless.

I'm a big picture person—I'm not big on the details—so if someone suggests that the only way to go is to get immersed in the details I know that won't work for me. I worked hard to learn about the business. I watched what other businesses like mine were doing and I questioned if it would work in my restaurant, would it work in my geographical area, and would it work with my customers? The people who live in rural Maine are very different from the residents of New York City. I had to decide what advice I could use and what would not help me at all.

There is a lot of trial and error in the beginning. You do something and you feel it out. Does it feel like it is working for you or not? If it's not working, then decide why. Is it because you're not good at it yet? Would further training help bring you into your comfort zone? Speaking of training, when we stop learning we stop growing. Training ourselves is as important as training any employee.

Reading was also a vital component—not only as a way to learn but to create a space and enjoy the mental relaxation of a good book.

Development should never stop. I'm always in the process of learning and evolving; it's an ongoing challenge. Journaling was an excellent path to help me kick-start my journey to understanding feelings and challenges. I started journaling in 1999 and discovered that by journaling (daily if possible) I had the opportunity to see my life from a different perspective. I could see how I would react to different situations. In the process of journaling I would realize how I would have done something better or what decisions I would have made to help me feel better about what was happening.

I started journaling when my husband was dying of cancer. I had a business partner, a 300-hundred-seat restaurant, and eighty employees. To say I had more than enough on my plate and that life was difficult is putting it lightly. Staying focused was a monumental task and writing helped me keep life in perspective. I needed a way to record what was happening and writing helped me to identify the myriad of feelings I was experiencing.

Considering all the pressures, I was surprised to discover the abundant joy I had. I recognized it and celebrated it. I realized how crucial it was to stay positive and focus on hope. I realized early on that success begins in our minds.

In the beginning of my business there was no thought of failure—never. It never entered my mind, it wasn't an option. I knew very little about the restaurant business so I concentrated on learning as much as I could about the business, not about what might happen if I didn't get it right. I was so busy learning that there was no time for negativity; I was excited—scared but excited. I envisioned people dining and loving the food and that's what happened.

As I went through new challenges I had to learn new ways to bring in new information. I was learning how to be an excellent patient advocate while doing what I could for my business partner and the restaurant.

After eighteen years and the death of my sister and my husband, we decided to lease the restaurant business. Two and a half years later they failed and closed the business. Since we owned the real estate, we made a conscious decision to re-open the restaurant again. It wasn't a path I would have chosen. We have since sold the property and moved on to other careers we have passion for. Life and time also changed our priorities. It was time to move on.

I believe we have an active role in creating our future. Jack Canfield teaches it in his "Success Principles." It is a crucial tool to help stay focused on the positives of tomorrow. It's just too easy to focus on the negatives and a little help on the positive angle couldn't hurt!

Wright

What do you feel is the most dynamic reason for your success?

Fazio

It would definitely be my ability to believe in tomorrow. I don't know if you remember Scarlet O'Hara in *Gone with the Wind*, but I think she had something going for herself.

Wright

She was southern wasn't she?

Fazio

She was a southern belle. She would always put her hand on her forehead and say, "I can't think about this today, I just can't. I'm going to think about this tomorrow." Tomorrow always brings a different perspective to the subject, unless you beat the subject to death today and are stuck in what "is" and not in what it could be. Life is life—some of us have more obstacles than others. I think I have had my fair share and if I concentrated on the tragedies I would never be able to move forward.

When I was two and a half years old I was nearly burned to death. It was a terrible accident; I spilled five gallons of hot soup. One third of my body suffered third degree burns. The scars were thick and ugly and kids are cruel. When other children would see me, they would recoil in disgust and make terrible faces. My parents persisted with the skin grafting operations and eventually the scaring was brought down to a minimum. It was a powerful life lesson that things get better with time and being proactive is an important part of the process.

That was just the beginning. By the age of twenty my house had burned down, my father had died of a heart attack, and my mother had died of cancer. You might say keeping a positive attitude was not a simple task. What I did learn was you can't concentrate on injustice and stay positive at the same time—I picked positive. You can only serve one master, so I picked hope. I searched out the possibilities and tuned out the daily dismal reality. Just in case we don't have our own dismal reality, we can count on the media to feed us plenty. I wanted more of, "I'm going to think about that tomorrow." I always believed it was going to be good and that it would only get better—it did. Our life goes where our mind takes us.

Wright

How do you see rules for life translating into life and business achievements?

Fazio

Rules? I have been known to break one or two rules along the way (I think it comes with the entrepreneur spirit); but I also believe we need structure too. I think sometimes we see rules as harsh and unyielding but I believe most of us need some structure and guidelines to keep us focused. If I'm following guidelines, they need to be specific.

Often my structure comes in the form of values: don't lie, cheat, or steal. Integrity is a vital part of my existence. First I had to discover what my values were, and then I had to live by them and be accountable. Truth is an important value to live by; besides, telling the truth is just far easier on the memory. You don't have to reconstruct the truth, you don't have remember the truth; but you have to remember a lie. Some of us have a bad memory; the truth works out better.

I love being straight with people, it usually throws them completely off guard. So many people are ready for the canned response or the staged answers. Honesty and straight talk can be disarming. You can see it in their faces. They usually look at you with big eyes and say, "Oh, really?" It's also refreshing for people to just hear from somebody who is not playing any games. Life is pretty straightforward when you are true to your values.

Wright

Who do you think influenced you to grow and push yourself further?

Fazio

In the beginning there was really no one to push me or mentor me, so I rented one. I call it the "Rent-A-Mentor Program." Listen and learn and Jack Canfield's "Self Esteem and Peak Performance" was probably the first educational tape series I heard. I spent hours listening to those tapes, sometimes over and over again.

Tapes don't change one's life but they changed the perspective of how I saw my life. The tapes gave me a whole new avenue of looking at life and were a new tool of listening and learning. Hearing Stephen Covey tapes and reading his book also had a profound influence on me.

When the student is ready the teacher appears. Here I am, nine years into my business and I hear Stephen Covey talk about "climbing the ladder of success only to have it leaning against the wrong wall." That one line alone made me stand up and take notice. Whose dream was I working for? People would say what a wonderful restaurant I had, but was it *my* dream? Was it *my* passion? People were my passion but the restaurant business wasn't. Something inside of me wanted more and since I didn't come from a business background or a competitive working environment I started to search for more information. I wondered how I could take the experience I had and do something I was passionate about.

I didn't have the time or the inclination to commit to a college course. I discovered seminars, educational CDs, and tapes. I listened to tapes and read books by gurus like Jack Canfield, Stephen Covey, Tom Miller, and many more.

I started the quest for knowledge when I compared myself to other businesspeople. I was doing as well as they were but I lacked the confidence. I felt like I was missing something. I had a good business and I couldn't see and appreciate my own success. I couldn't see in me what others saw. That probably was a blessing because it kept my mind open and gave me the willingness to listen to others with more experience. Yes, I did a lot of things right. I made a lot of customers happy and created a wonderful place to gather; but I needed to listen, read, and learn, and expand my mind, understanding that I didn't know all the answers and was not expected to. That helped change my personal views of myself. I have learned from the best and I aspire to pass along a message of changing destructive self-talk and encouraging others to learn to appreciate their work and accomplishments.

There is plenty of opportunity around us, it's consistently there, but we have to open up our minds and look for it. Then our challenge is to believe that we can have it and accept it. Sometimes people see opportunity and say, "Yeah, but not for me." They don't recognize what they've already accomplished. We all need a little help to nudge us to take other steps, to learn a little more, think outside the box, and, in some cases just throw the box away.

Wright

Is balance in life something you think people should be concerned with?

Fazio

Absolutely. Today more than ever, having balance in our lives is the only thing that will ultimately keep us sane, especially if we are in business for ourselves. I spent the first fifteen years in my business taking care of everyone else's needs—my customers, my employees, my business partner, and the lenders. I believed I was taking care of my children's needs by providing for them and creating some financial security by building my business.

I finally came to the incredible realization that there isn't enough money to compensate for quality time with family. The important people in my life, whether they are my children, spouse, siblings, or best friends, need to be with me and I need to be with them. We need people around us who share our faith and honor who we are. I realize now that balance is not just quiet time, it's not just time alone, but it's also social time with people I care about. All work and no play makes me cranky (forget "makes a dull boy")—it just makes people ornery. Take time for the fun stuff and if you don't have fun in your life, create it!

Wright

If there was one message you could share with the world, what would it be?

Fazio

I think it would be good to take a minute or two every morning before you hit the ground running to consciously ask yourself, "If today was it—the last day I had to live—how would I live it? What actions would I take to help create the future for the ones I leave behind?" The question is different than, "If today was my last day, what would I do?" One question addresses you and your needs, the other addresses what you will leave behind. Would you go into the office if it were your last day? I don't think so.

I personally would find my grandchildren and spend time with them. I'd call my daughter, hug my son, and connect with my brothers and sister. It's more about what can I give them to remember. If today was the only day that I had to complete a promise or create a memory, that is what I would spend time on.

It's not just about my personal desires but how I lived life. It is how a person lives completely that will create a legacy. In reality, we only have today. You don't get to think about it. We all have the same twenty-four hours. Some of us waste those twenty-four hours, some of us make the most of them, and the rest of us are in between.

I realized how precious time is when my sister was on the phone one day planning to visit me and the next day she was dead from a brain aneurism. Fortunately and gratefully, the last time we saw each other we had talked on a deeper level and shared how much we loved each other. You don't get another shot at it, you don't get to say, "Oh wait, I forgot one thing—." You get a new chance every day to make things right, so take advantage of it.

A person has to decide what quality time is. If spending time with my dog because I really like my dog and he makes me happy (not that I would have a dog now because dogs never learn to prepare their own dinners), then that is a day well spent. I have learned to pick something that makes me feel good and honor it.

My children were eleven and thirteen years old when I got started in the restaurant business. I cannot begin to tell you how many games and concerts I missed, along with family gatherings. Sometimes we look for excuses to avoid family gatherings and that's too bad. We don't realize how important they are to our own life blood; even if we think they are annoying. They are probably annoying because we are seeing some mirror images of ourselves and they become obvious at family celebrations.

I happen to like my family and the more tied up I was with business and the more I realized I was letting precious time slip through my fingers, the more I searched for a solution. I eventually realized there was a solution. I had to trust people around me to take over when I needed to leave and I needed to help them feel good about being trusted to be in charge. Here comes the hard part: then I had to accept the way they took charge. You see, once I gave it to them, I had to trust that they would be okay and so would my business. They might not do it exactly the way I would do it—they may not make the exact same decisions—but I accepted the tradeoff because I got something in return. I was balancing out my life and giving my employees a chance to grow in self-confidence. People forget that in most cases someone else making decisions for them will not dramatically change the course of their future, especially if it is for one or two hours or even a few days. Everything can be corrected. And just because I'm there won't insure a mistake-free environment.

A full life can be created if we let others do something that they may be good at. My challenge today is to make every day count for me and for anybody who comes in contact with me.

Wright

What a great conversation. I really do appreciate your taking all this time to answer these questions. It's been fascinating. I've learned a lot and I'm sure our readers will.

Fazio

If I may add one thing David: I started to change my perspective on the small stuff. I let go of small things and when the world didn't crumble I was able to trust the natural order of things. I felt safe in resigning from running the universe. Then I had some fun with it, like holding a door open for somebody else, looking the person in the eye, and smiling at him or her.

I was born and raised in New York and when I'm in New York, I do this; it's just fun to see their shocked faces. We seem to be too busy to take those five seconds to connect and when I get a smile back, I know I've just done something good. If you smile at somebody, it's almost guaranteed you'll get a smile in return. Find small ways to connect, it is so worth it. Like going through a tollbooth and paying for the car behind you. Have you ever done that?

Wright

Never, I should I guess.

Fazio

The first time it happened to me I was confused, "how come?" was my first response and then it slid into a pleasant surprise and a tiny renewal of faith in life. This isn't about doing for someone else. I've learned that whatever I give, I get ten-fold in return.

I ask people in my audiences, "Have you taken the time to look at your own successes and celebrate your own achievements?" Seldom is there a resounding Yes! People don't take the time to celebrate who they are. What will you do from this point on to create a positive chain of events? What actions will to take to move forward? What is one thing you will do today to make tomorrow better?

Wright

I appreciate this conversation and I applaud your success. You've made it through some pretty hard times and I appreciate that.

Fazio

I heard this thought a while ago and I'd like to leave it with you: "When your life flashes before you, make sure you're going to enjoy the movie."

About the Author

ANNETTE FAZIO'S twenty-five years of leadership experience in the food service business renders her a unique restaurant and business owner.

Annette's infectious, quick-witted humor, creativity, and personality complement her professionalism. Annette built Fazio's Italian Restaurant from the ground up and created the mainstay recipes.

Annette is a graduate of the Professional Chef's Program at the Cambridge School of Culinary Arts in Cambridge, Massachusetts, and serves on the board of alumni. Annette has hosted a cable television cooking show in the Boston area, has served on the Advisory Board of the Seacoast Career Schools, and has been an instructor of Continuing Education classes at Le Cordon Bleu.

Annette believes her success is a combination of treating people well, spending ample amount of time in the kitchen making sure the restaurant lived up to the Fazio name, serving the best Italian food, and offering personal homespun service: "... *just-a like-a you mammas.*"

Annette Fazio
The Restaurant Diva
P.O. Box 371
York, Maine 03909
Phone: 207.363.3162
E-mail: annette@annettefazio.com
www.therestaurantdiva.com

Chapter 9

Traci Totino

THE INTERVIEW

David Wright (Wright)

Today we are talking with Traci Totino. She has earned a bachelor's, a master's, and a doctorate degree in Communication. She has been dedicated to serving employers and associates nationwide through intellectually challenging and personalized programs of instruction and service. Traci has over eleven years of management, public speaking, and entrepreneurial experience. She has developed several training programs on leadership, coaching, train the trainer, supervisory skills, and team and personal development on how to master success. She has trained, developed, and presented to all levels of corporate employees. Traci has authored several articles and has been the featured speaker at many events.

You certainly are qualified to talk about success, considering your background. So, tell our readers how you define success.

Traci Totino (Totino)

Success is a personal measurement. Success doesn't necessarily equate to material goals and gains. As a child, success is tying your shoes for the first time, and graduating grade school or getting married may qualify as a success as one ages.

For myself, I employ methods pertaining to goal completion and satisfaction. I will put a new goal out into the Universe. From there, I qualify a measurement of what I term a win. For example, within the next six weeks I will have secured ten new clients and have met someone with whom my company can strategically align. Once I reach the standard that I set for myself, I often surpass it, creating a benchmark for my win. After six weeks, I've secured fifteen new clients and three new peers. This then becomes success.

I speak for myself, but I am certain many of you will agree that our worst critic is usually ourselves. I am by far the most difficult person I have to please. I play mini-games with myself and I don't tolerate losing against me. I remain in a positive state of mind and I release all worry and fear.

I continue to hone my desire, belief, and expectancy behaviors as taught to me by Jose Silva. I embrace challenge and competition while keeping my eye on my goal and acting with kindness. You cannot allow others to define your successes. If these ideals do not belong to you, personal fulfilment will be lacking. What one person may define as success, another may deem to be mediocrity or even failure.

To succeed at a task can be as simple as achieving a goal, whether it's been explicitly planned for or not. The only measure of success is that which can be measured against what you set for yourself.

Success is living well. Success is being healthy. Success is going to work for pleasure not necessity. Success is freedom. Success is easy to attain. Success is so very personal.

Wright

I have read several things by Jose Silva and appreciate his work. You mentioned you were taught by Silva. What impact did his training have on you?

Totino

Jose Silva positively impacted and changed my life. He was a brilliant man and masterful teacher. Once I began looking at the world through the teachings of Jose Silva, new possibilities opened to me and I realized that everything was attainable—personally and professionally. Banishing negativity, previously aimed both inward and outward, allowed me to see life with fresh perspective where I was in control and could positively affect my future.

I stumbled upon his book, *The Silva Mind Control Method,* in early 1997. At this point in my life I had earned my master's degree and was due to complete my doctorate in one year's time. I was an adjunct professor at a local university and I felt overwhelmed by the confusion as to what I truly wanted to be "when I grew up." I knew that being a professor would present a ceiling or limitation to my earning potential but I still traveled down that path. I was at the university library choosing a book for my students to read when out of nowhere I literally tripped on a book that had fallen before me—it was Silva's book.

This is Silva's message: We can attain anything we want in our lives to include material wealth, good health, and happiness with ease of being. There are four "rules" or "methods" presented to attain personal successes. The first is to desire the object or condition. Desire is a matter of yearning and thirsting for this gift. The second is to believe it can transpire. This method will only work if what you desire can be achieved.

I often disclose a personal example to friends/colleagues regarding the art of believing and why this is crucial to success. I desire for my deceased dog to be with me, alive and well, but despite my intentional desire, it cannot be achieved. Therefore I do not believe it will happen so I will not waste my energy on the desire. Keep your desires believable and they will become your reality.

With my example I have revealed the third step in the process of achieving complete success—one must expect to receive the gift. Expectancy must be visual and promoted with energy or feeling.

The first two steps, desire and belief, are active because you are in control. But expectancy is passive and in my opinion, the most difficult step. You must allow the powers of the Universe to bring to you that which you desire and believe. There is nothing more you can do but wait, never losing sight of that which you've requested. Through visualization and active mediation, you will achieve your desired outcome.

And the last rule or step in the process according to Silva, which I deem also very important, is that you must never use your mindpower for negativity or for harm. Ultimately, your bad wishes will come back to you. I mentioned earlier that I embrace my competitors and always act in kindness because ultimately my good wishes come back to me.

Wright

Let's talk about negativity for a minute. To what degree do negative influences that enter our minds prevent us from accomplishing our goals and being successful?

Totino

Negativity has absolutely no place in one's life. Omit negative words, ideas, or thoughts from your world. They serve no good purpose. I know this may seem difficult. As an expert, it is difficult for me at times. Any thought or vision to which you give energy will transpire despite whether it's negative or positive, therefore you should only think positively. By allowing negative thoughts into our minds we cannot help allowing doubt to creep in, and doubt begets worry, causing us to spiral into a vicious cycle of negativity.

To achieve our goals in life we must focus our positive energy to make these goals our new successes. Imagine a still pond. At the start of a task the pond is full of clear water, representing our positive energy that we're devoting to accomplishing our task. Introducing negative energy into our thinking is like adding a piece of algae. Left unchecked this weed would slowly grow and cover the surface of the pond, suffocating the once clean, clear water below. Negativity is like the algae and if given the opportunity will engulf our once positive thinking—our good intentions and best efforts will be snuffed out by fear, worry, and insecurity. It has been proven by ancient sages that the Universal Law of Attraction will deliver to you that which you think, speak, and see. If you are feeling melancholy, sad, or angry, you will attract those situations, which will amplify these emotions. Conversely, if you are feeling happy, content, and joyful, situations that amplify these emotions will present themselves.

Another really important action we must take is to not fear what might come. Fear will ultimately hold you back. If you don't attempt something new, how will you ever know whether or not it could have been attained? All great inventions, events, and relationships have begun with one single thought from one single person. If Gates and Lincoln could attain success (and since we're all created equal), why can't you? Confidence is key. Confidence in oneself, the Universe, the laws of attraction and reciprocity, and confidence in other people we will meet along the way will bring completion and satisfaction in our success journeys.

If we think about our perfect house—a house we desire to own— and with intent we visualize it, we have to rely on our self-confidence that what we imagine will most certainly become our reality. Once we have a clear picture in our mind, complete with visual, tactile, olfactory, and auditory senses, we are one step closer to making that picture become our reality. When we incorporate fear into our process of attaining success, we undo what we've set out to create.

Wright

How do you turn a negative mood into a positive mood? Why is this important?

Totino

When feeling sad, angry, fearful, worried, or any other negative emotion, it is imperative for your greater good to alter your emotions. You are in complete control of yourself, therefore you are responsible for changing your frowns to smiles and your tears into laughter. Think for a moment how you feel when your laugh or hear good news, embrace a child or pet, a spouse or companion, see the sunshine or drink a cold glass of water on a scorching summer day? Activities such as these evoke happiness and ease on our bodies and minds. The emotional result is that of pure and positive universal energy. This positive energy is in line with balance and calm, which translates into abundance and prosperity as set forth by the Universe.

I've read and subsequently experienced throughout my years of studies that if our energy is not tuned in with the Universe, we will be unable to grasp our desires. My favourite analogy is that of a radio station. If you select a specific channel on your radio, it is impossible to hear the broadcast of a different station. So let's apply that example to our success procedure. When yearning for a better job, a life partner, to lose weight, quit smoking, have more money, or anything else, we have to set our internal "station" to match the frequency of the Universe. Our internal station to achieve success is the one that is tuned in for positivism, confidence, courage, belief in oneself, and gratitude.

Wright

I've been positive and have stayed happy and kind, however, sometimes really bad things still happen, how do you explain this?

Totino

As humans we must believe there is a much stronger power or entity that protects and guides us. If we believe this to be true in our heart of hearts, when negative things happen we must believe it's for our greater good. Negativity is your perception due to the opposition of what you might have fancied, however, this higher power (some call God, others refer to as guardian angels, whatever name you assign) is a powerful energy that has your best interest at hand. What we as people deem negative will in fact be positive. We mustn't fight the energy or be resistant; rather, go with it and make the best of what's before us. We must have blind faith that the result of the unfavorable situation will result in greater happiness.

I will give you an example: I have a friend who owned a very successful consulting firm. She disliked it although it brought her great monetary rewards. She spoke with disdain about the agency that governed her company and often admitted the politics were creating a life of misery. Not long after her rants, the Universe answered her wish and her company was subject to much criticism, nearly putting her out of business. With this news came worry and fear and much uncertainty regarding her future. Weeks passed and there was no cessation of these accusations; she became worn out and almost surrendered.

I was with her when she met a woman we now know was her "Earth Guide." It was no accident that we were at the right place at the right time—fate had brought Janet into both our lives. Janet is an artist but was born with keen psychic abilities. What transpired next has completely strengthened my belief in a higher intelligence.

We were speaking with Janet about her artwork when she glared at my friend and told her to not be resistant to what the Universe was offering—do not be saddened or worried—instead, embrace the change and the uncertainty and realize full well that the Universe has a better plan. She then said the guardian angels were in the bleachers, on the sidelines watching. We were shocked and astonished. We kept silent for most of the day until we both realized she was right.

My friend is still unsure about what will become of her consulting firm but she has been working on a new project that she enjoys. This new endeavour has instilled joy and focus and she is confident. When we talk these days, she laughs and tells me about the new Earth Guides that are presented to her every day. She's regained control of her emotions and her well-being and is expecting things will be more satisfying than before.

The Universe wants us to be happy, to have abundance and solace; it does not want us to suffer or be without that which we desire.

When our energy is not in line with Universal Energy, occurrences take place to force us back in line. These occurrences may not feel good, they may cause great discomfort for a short time, however, the choice is ours to resist and fight or allow the discomfort to ultimately resolve our balance.

Wright

Why is gratitude important for success?

Totino

Regarding the friend I just mentioned who has the successful consulting firm, besides learning the value of positive thinking and patience, she also learned about gratitude and appreciation. She had a great business that brought her many rewards. Instead of praising and being thankful for these gifts, she took for granted the riches that had been bestowed upon her. When the riches ceased to flow, she realized how thankful she should have been.

Since meeting Janet, we both are thankful for all we have. Gratitude is humbling. Gratitude is key to receiving those desires for which we ask. If you continuously gave someone gifts and never heard a "thank you," you might begin to wonder if that person was ungrateful or was taking advantage of you. The same principle is true for life and the Universe.

I like to refer to gratitude and thankfulness as keys to unlocking treasures. Think of something for which you feel appreciation. If the appreciation is genuine, the thought will evoke contentment and happiness. If you find yourself dwelling on the negativity in your moment, become mindful of the things everyone too often takes for granted—the everyday abilities, opportunities, relationships, and possessions we have. For example, whether it is physical functions such as sight or sound or our innate capabilities or having close family or friends or having a place to sleep and clothes on our back, we should be continuously aware of these gifts because some people lack them. When one seeks this path of appreciation, the emotions emitted from self are those in tune with the greater universal energy aligned with abundance and prosperity.

Wright

Most people have told me that visualization is very difficult, but most trainers say it is extremely important as a tool. Would you explain visualization to our readers?

Totino

Visualization is possibly one of the most powerful tools we have in our personal armoury. It allows us to dictate the path our lives will take—not each step necessarily, but the course heading we'll take. An example I often rely on to explain the powers of the mind is the lemon visual: Close your eyes and imagine a lemon. See its vibrant yellow rind and now pick it up and smell it. Take a knife and cut it down the middle and visualize clearly the juices seeping out, dripping onto the table. Now pick up half the lemon and bite into it. I will guarantee, if done correctly, your mouth will be watering. This is just how powerful your mind is. Your subconscious mind does not differentiate between fantasy and reality and does not calculate or measure time as we've been taught.

Attainment of goals relies heavily on imagination. I invite you to sit back and imagine your desired scenario, focusing on a successful outcome. A few minutes during the day or before retiring to sleep, close your eyes and picture the ideal scene of your success. If you want the perfect house, picture walking up the path, the color of the shingles, and the number of steps up to the door. Smell the flowers in the garden; bend down and pick up a flower. Now walk into your home. In your thoughts, create as much detail as you are able. Are there steps? How many? Are they wood or concrete? Walk inside your dream home. What does it look like? What does it feel like to walk through each room? Is the sun shining through the kitchen window? Are there tiled floors or hardwood? What does the fresh paint smell like? You can go further, picturing entertaining your friends and family, and your first holiday.

When you build your mental masterpiece of attainment, you are nearly there; all that happens next is for that period of time to catch up with your actual time! This is active mediation or dynamic thinking. Since our minds are so powerful, we can literally imagine or visualize a scenario, a person, a result in clear detail. Tap into all of your senses as if this wish has already occurred. I love dynamic visualization, as it is my own mental holiday from everyday stress and tasks.

Wright

You've told us about universal energy, visualization, and emotion control. What practical advice can you offer regarding the attainment of success?

Totino

The first, most important practicality, in my opinion, is to seize every opportunity that is set before you. When you ask the Universe for anything, in return, this Energy is lining up that which you need to gain fulfilment. If you stay tuned in, you will begin to notice it in your life path—people, events, items, and ideas will be thrust upon you. Do not be resistant; rather, accept and explore each prospect. Of all the people you will meet, one of them may be the perfect ally to catapult your desire into success. Trusted alliances facilitate the journey as the work is shared among many. Additionally, you will be introduced to other contacts who may be helpful.

This design is not meant only for business practices but also personal aspirations. For example, my friend Pat had a meeting with an associate on September 11, 2001, at Windows of the World at nine in the morning. Days before, another client had changed an appointment to Wednesday, the twelfth. Instead of traveling into the city two days consecutively, Pat had decided to meet them both on the twelfth. She doesn't think it was a premonition; rather, an internal force that had been tuned in to a higher intelligence. This higher self guided her to accept the appointment on Wednesday and change the Tuesday appointment as opposed to the reverse. This is only one example of similar occurrences.

Another example: I was third in line in a retail store where the cashier was having a hard time with her current customer. Those behind me were getting restless and the gentleman in front of me was beginning to show signs of annoyance. He turned to me and rolled his eyes in contempt. Instead of allowing the timely wait to impede on my good mood, I smiled at the man and offered a simple scenario—we could've been outside in the blistering heat rather than where we were, in an air-conditioned building. He returned my smile and we began to chat. The conversation resulted in a profitable relationship and a new friendship. This man had been president of an international hospitality corporation. He wound up hiring my company to facilitate training in all of their locations. This is one ideal example of turning a negative situation into something positive.

Wright

What role does desire play in the in the pursuit of success and happiness, and would you give us an example?

Totino

Without desire we have only a minimal chance of attaining goals. Imagine a high jumper staring at the bar set at a new height for the first time. When looking at that bar he or she must want to hit that new height more than anything, more than the risk of injury, more than the fear of failing, more than anything in the world. At that point in time the person must desire to achieve that new goal above all else.

The same applies for everyday life—not only do you have to desire something, you must desire it and *believe* that what you desire is attainable. Desire and visualization go hand in hand. Before you can visualize your future you have to know what it is that you want—what you *really* want. When you have the outcome in your mind, an outcome that you really want, then you can use the visualization technique. Every step down the road brings your goal that one step closer until it's almost just a formality of reaching out and touching it.

Many find difficulty in controlling their own mind. When we have that commitment to our destination, it's a case of closing our eyes and picturing what it'll be like when we get there—what we'll see, touch, taste, smell, the position of every tree, shrub, and pathway. By the time we start, our mind is already halfway there; the physical act of walking the pathways is almost an inconvenience and the journey a little more than a set of mundane and routine steps, always keeping the goal in mind.

Wright

I don't know what to think about karma. It seems a little mystical to me; however, there are many great thinkers as well as intelligent people who believe in karma. Would you tell me what it is and how I can use it?

Totino

As with many things we've already covered, karma is inextricably linked with other ideas. When we talked about forming alliances to "spread the wealth," that's very much at the core of the idea of karma. One of the principles is familiar to us all—"what goes around comes around." So, by using the idea of strategically aligning with other companies or individuals, not only does it make sound financial sense, but also in wider terms we balance the universe. Essentially we're saying that by helping others—sharing your good fortune—they in turn will share with us.

Thinking personally, if you have a hot stock tip for example, are you more likely to tell the person who did you a good turn and referred a client, or the colleague who's only out for herself or himself? The same is true in reverse—we've all been on the receiving end of "sharp" practices in life, and it's human nature to wish to take revenge—even if only for a moment. I've always been a big believer in karma, and in these situations, even though the benefit may not be immediately apparent, the Universe will not only reward good behavior, but will hand out relevant punishment to the other party.

Thinking about personal examples again, the person who stole a client from you is just as likely to have been as underhanded to another colleague or acquaintance. Ever heard of the saying that "you meet the same people coming down as you did going up?" Well, that's karma—you can't tread on people to get to the top and think that when you hit a rocky patch and start to slide that those people will have forgotten—at the very least you'll get no favors.

Wright

What are some of the tools you consider to be part of reaching success?

Totino

We are all equipped with the tools we need for our personal successes. First you start with a yearning or desire for your goal, then you must believe, relinquishing all doubt, that your desire will become your reality. Lastly, you must expect the desire to be brought to your life. As you begin to think, dream, and speak about your goals, the wheels are in motion to create the end result.

Part of success is having a good team of someone else or of many people. If your goal requires ten people, the Universe will ensure these people enter your life. If you stay on track with your imagery and determination, each new event or person introduced to you will be part of the plan to achievement.

Do not give up. It is so cliché to report the importance of determination but determination is essential to achieving success. I will give you a credible example—one of a multitude I have experienced. I was seeking a new bank with certain criteria for my business checking account. I had been searching for a few days and to my dismay, none of the financial institutions offered what I required. I found myself at the shopping center in town that evening. While fourth in line to make my purchase, the cashier was having problems with an un-ticketed item. The lag in service stirred up some anger and frustration among the other customers.

Rather than become annoyed, I began an innocent conversation with the woman in front of me. I had asked her a question regarding the weather—a simple conversation starter and frankly, a pleasant way to pass time. She eagerly began to tell me about her longer than usual ride to work that morning due to the heavy rains. She continued to rant that her hair was disheveled and she was late to meet with a prominent investor.

The word "investor" prompted me to ask what she does at work. With luck being no part of this scenario, she answered, "I'm the president of a new branch of a bank." I told her what I had been seeking for my business finances and she was able to oblige. I waited for her to complete her purchase and she waited for me. We exited the store together, chit-chatting about everything and anything. I had found an answer to my "request" and also a new friendship. We happened to have parked near one another so I walked to her car to attain a business card.

We said our goodbyes and as I turned away, she blurted, "What were the chances we'd meet?" I turned back, smiled at her coyly, and replied, "100 percent." There was a 100 percent chance I'd meet a person, see a commercial, or stumble upon an Internet site that would provide what I had requested.

To date she and I have done great business together. It was not an accident I met Clara that day. The cultivation of a mutually beneficial relationship was cast upon both of us by the arrangement of a higher source. The Law of Attraction continuously proves its power.

Wright

I have always been fascinated by the "Laws of Attraction," however, I'm not sure I really understand the concept. Would you tell me how I can develop it as a tool for success?

Totino

If 1,000 people tell you there is a law that exists and has been proven, you may find it difficult to believe, especially if this law is one you cannot see or touch. Similar to the law of gravity that cannot physically be seen or felt, it must be accepted on blind faith. We know the law of gravity is real because any doubt is abolished once you test it. Throw a ball into the air and that ball will fall to the earth. The Law of Attraction is also unseen, yet many millions of people have tested its validity to find that it truly and undoubtedly is.

The Law of Attraction can be best understood as that which is like unto itself is drawn. This law is based upon the frequency of energy, emotions, or thoughts that are emitted will be returned in matching feelings or ideas. For example, if you worry about getting into a car accident, the repetitive thought of a crash will be sent into the Universe. According the Law of Attraction, it is very likely you will be involved in a crash-like catastrophe. Luckily, people can attract wonderful occurrences and gifts into their lives also. The principle is simple to understand. Whatever you think, imagine, and feel will be brought to you in matching results.

I am able to give you a plethora of examples; however, there are two occurrences that I deliberately attracted into my life for the purpose of my professional and personal successes. I had been diagnosed with a cancer-like condition that was given a 100 percent possibility to reappear once it had been removed. At first I was nervous and scared and my dreadful thoughts began to control my every moment. I contacted an attorney for the purposes of drawing up my will. I began to plan for my terrible future. I would fall asleep at night picturing my demise.

Days before the scheduled medical procedure, I went to a local bookstore. I found a book in the self-help section titled, *Excuse Me, Your Life is Waiting* by Lynn Grabhorn. I began reading it that same afternoon, unaware that her words would change my life. I realized the author's message that I had known all along—through fear, I had suppressed my own inner knowledge and beliefs. As I thumbed impatiently through each page, I took control of my own life, my body, my health, and my condition. Through emotion and thought I relayed the message and feeling of perfect health and wellness to myself.

Each day prior to the doctor's visit, I concentrated on feeling good and being completely self-confident that the cancer cells would be removed and never return. Years have passed since the minor surgery and, as required, I've been to my doctor for an exam every few months. My doctor is amazed. He is almost in disbelief that the cancer has not returned. He assures me it will be back but I know it will not. Through the Law of Attraction one can summon good health if one's state of mind or vibrating energy matches that of healthiness.

In my professional endeavors, the Law of Attraction has brought me countless successes. My favorite experience was a meeting, planned by the Universe, with a woman who would become my mentor and friend. Due to this encounter, I started a business at the age of twenty-one that became an empire in less than two years.

I was a graduate student at a local university and was asked to substitute for a professor who was unable to teach her class. I was inexperienced and hadn't even completed my master's degree, so I was also struggling with self-confidence. I agreed to the task, as this professor had become an acquaintance through many hours of my time in academia.

I instructed the class with ease that evening, earning the respect and accolades of the students who attended. Months later, the same professor was contracted to teach a corporate class for a very prominent insurance company. One day prior, she had to cancel due to a family emergency. Although the Communication Department was privy to my scarce teaching experience, the Business Department only knew I was a graduate assistant with only a bachelor's degree and no corporate experience. With this knowledge, the Dean of the department asked me to meet with her regarding the scheduled training for the following day. This one meeting would be the catapult of my career as an educator. After a brief conversation with "Dr. Mom," as she became known to me, I agreed to facilitate the training for 349 individuals at the Nassau Coliseum in Long Island, New York.

I remember arriving early in the morning to be greeted by the Vice President. My palms were sweaty, my heart was racing, my mouth was dry and I was more nervous than I had ever been. At eight in the morning, I was the first instructor. My responsibility was to motivate the group of sales agents and teach them about diversity and respect. I was the youngest person in the room by at least a decade. Earning their confidence and admiration would be difficult but I prevailed. Of the 349 evaluations I received, 348 of them had given me "ten out of ten." Amusingly, the final evaluation had given me high marks but was critical of my age. I guess this particular student didn't fully embrace the message I was teaching. Prior to leaving for the day, the Vice President approached me and offered me a contract to repeat my performance nationwide. That was my start.

In hindsight, I realized I had asked the Universe to reveal and provide my career path. Each night before bed, I visualized myself as powerful and wealthy, yet humble and helpful. I had no idea what would transpire until The Law of Attraction brought me what I had desired. Not everyone will believe in this Law but I ask those who are in doubt to experiment with it. The results will not only be amazing but will undoubtedly yield prosperity, abundance, and greatness.

Wright

Any final thoughts that you would like to share with our readers that might help them be more successful in their business and personal lives?

Totino

Connect with yourself first and really learn to like yourself. Befriend yourself. Don't blame yourself if you feel depressed or angry; be gentle with your thoughts. You are your only direct connection with the Universe. That in turn is the vehicle to transport your desires to you. Compliment your strengths and be lenient with your weaknesses.

Respect and be kind to all living things. We do not inhabit the world alone. We have intertwined energies that will ultimately affect our lives. We are taught the Golden Rule and ought to heed this teaching. When we give without the expectation of reward, we find abundance is then granted.

Thirdly, keep control over your brain. Since the mind is so powerful, when left out of control it can wreak havoc. Emotions are the source of our power. Throughout history, it is evident that negative emotions have initiated war, self-sacrifice, and even death. However, it is also known that positive emotions have resulted in successes. Try to maintain a state of happiness, confidence, and humility. When you're feeling sad, lonely, bored, annoyed, or angry, resurrect a favorable experience that evokes calmness and joy.

Alter your state of thinking and do not lose sight of your goals. Visualize several times a day in great detail that which you desire. Convince yourself you've already attained success, then expect it to unfold before you. Take a break and experience a mental holiday free from stress and problems.

Maintain total control of your mind at all times. Do not allow your intrusive thoughts to hinder your beliefs or desires. Do not allow other people to negatively influence your dreams, thus deterring you from moving ahead.

Lastly, remember that happiness and success are so very personal. While pursuing your goals, do not intentionally hurt or cause harm to anyone or anything. Push forward with unstoppable drive and relentless determination.

About the Author

TRACI TOTINO has earned a bachelor's, master's, and a doctorate degree in Communication. She has been dedicated to serving employers, associates, and individuals nationwide through intellectually challenging and personalized programs of instruction and service. Traci has over eleven years of management, public speaking, and entrepreneurial experience. She has developed several training programs on how to master success. She has presented to, trained, and developed all levels of corporate employees. Traci has been the featured speaker at many events—presenting in both English and Spanish.

Dr. Traci Totino has provided educational services and consulted for a number of major corporations (private and public), small businesses, not-for-profit, community and religious organizations, and educational institutions. In 1997, she launched TNT Educational Services (TNT). TNT is a training company that caters to corporate and personal success plans through assessment, training, and evaluation.

Dr. Totino remains an adjunct professor at William Paterson University. She has also taught both undergraduate and graduate classes for several other universities and colleges. She has written and published several articles relating to corporate culture and increased success in the home and workplace.

Dr. Totino has created the following educational materials:

- Learning projects for independent thinking
- Success strategies DVD & Workbook
- Training programs for self development
- Personal Growth DVDs
- Master trainer development
- Work and Life Balance
- Goal Attainment

Traci Totino
TNT Educational Services
24 Taylor Court
Parsippany, NJ 07054
Phone: 866.505.2073
E-mail: traci@tntedu.com
www.tntedu.com

Chapter 10

BRENT PATMOS

THE INTERVIEW

David Wright (Wright)

Brent Patmos is President and CEO of Perpetual Development Inc. He is an accomplished author with published works including *Insights to Leadership and Living, Driven to Sell, Success Talk,* and *Focus on Results.* Brent also holds the highest levels of certification as a Professional Behavioral and Values Analyst. His unique ability to define, process, and resolve complex sales situations into easily understood and actionable strategies have made him a sought-after expert in the areas of sales consulting, strategy, and development. Brent is also an accomplished speaker and foremost authority on the impact of behavioral assessment in sales selection, retention, and advanced performance. As a result, *Selling Power* magazine lists Perpetual Development among the top sales strategy and development companies in the United States. Brent is a professional member of the National Speakers Association and the International Speakers Network. He is a Paul Harris Fellow with Rotary International and holds numerous awards and recognitions for his achievements.

Brent, how has your passion for success changed during your career?

Brent Patmos (Patmos)

Passion around purpose and the passion for success have been an intense part of my life for as long as I can remember. It really is how God wired me. As a result of understanding and appreciating how I am wired, my definition of success has evolved and changed dramatically over the years, but my passion has remained intensely high.

I used to believe that success was the achievement of specific goals or specific outcomes that were primarily driven as an individual effort. This is important because I think many people define success as it relates to their individual effort, contribution, or result. What I have come to appreciate, both personally and professionally, is that success has as many definitions as there are people in the world. The common thread in keeping that passion for success high, regardless of the definition, is in identifying your specific passion, which generates your purpose, which inspires your performance, which drives your achievement and ultimately your success.

Here's a question that I ask professionally: are salespeople successful if they hit their numbers but dread every day they come to work? The answer is *no*. Regardless of the actual results, if an individual is wired for a completely different passion and purpose than the one he or she is fulfilling, then that person is behaviorally and motivationally misaligned.

Think about it. What happens when an individual's passion and purpose begin to erode or were never there in the first place? Results, achievement, and success are going to suffer. Success in a given endeavor, activity, or profession is predictable when behaviors and motivators are aligned with requirements and expectations. Change in my definition of success occurred for me when I deliberately reconnected my passion, my purpose, my behaviors, and my motivators. I like to call it my success alignment.

There are people who reside in all the valleys of their lives and they feel success is not attainable. They are in need of a success alignment. We all have to have the intestinal fortitude to do a little self-assessment from time to time and make sure our behaviors, motivators, passion, and purpose are working together to achieve at the level of our potential. This is what allows our passion for success to remain high throughout our careers even when each of us defines success differently.

Wright

Explain the concept of "Perpetual Development" and why you gave the name to your company.

Patmos

"Perpetual Development" was born out of the passion and the purpose that exists internally for helping others achieve their goals, recognize their successes, and really connect their passion and their purpose both personally and professionally.

I'm amazed that God made the human race to learn indefinitely. In their chosen careers, the most successful people leverage this ability for all it's worth. This means that they're committed to uninterrupted development. It's a part of who they are. The name Perpetual Development is rooted in the belief that a "never-ending" and "life-long" approach to learning, along with personal and professional development, is directly related to having an "expanded view." In this state of learning and development, individuals, companies, and organizations have the ability to see before others see, to see more than others see, see further than others see, achieve more than others achieve, and recognize that performance drives results.

The best athletes consistently analyze their performance with an absolute fervor and detail; the best salespeople do the same. They don't shrink from a crushing defeat—they rise up to the challenge. What they do is exploit it to uncover their own vulnerabilities and apply new learning to the next challenge. Successful people are not fair weather fans when it comes to their own development.

"Perpetual Development" is the kind of development worth investing in. For individuals as well as organizations it's that learning which develops and cultivates their mind while connecting their passion and their purpose. How well a salesperson, an organization, or anyone else is educated and developed is a reflection on their performance. That measurement, while it comes in results, is also measured in how well they have purposely developed their mind and in turn developed their skill. It translates in how well they think.

"Perpetual Development"—on-going never ending learning, never ending development—is a life-long passion because it forces us to deal with the reality that we can never become stale; we can never stagnate. We must always be growing, learning, and developing in some fashion. The name Perpetual Development was born out of the passion and the purpose to help others achieve their pinnacle of performance.

Wright

Brent, you have assessed, coached, and developed thousands of individuals, primarily salespeople. How do aspiring sales professionals define and pursue success?

Patmos

In many cases, success is defined by a single dimension: results. Personal and professional skills development is often neglected. Neglect occurs as a result of becoming consumed in low return sales activities. The salesperson determined to achieve maximum success learns that progress toward his or her development is really made one step at a time.

I equate it with building a house—you don't take the house and move it from blueprint to completion in a day; you're adding some concrete, you're adding a board, you're adding a brick, and every day there's a progression and another step forward. Salespeople should apply that focus and continue to grow and develop one brick at a time in the pursuit of their success.

Many salespeople become distracted, as I said earlier, by low return sales activities. The problem is they've given up on focusing any kind of time or effort on priorities of significance. One of the things I encourage people to do is to take time to think, plan, and do what I call "super thinking," a thirty-minute block of time with a focus on one specific topic. This super thinking time is really how aspiring sales professionals come to grips and get in contact with their definition of success and how they will pursue that success.

Research we've been involved with, dealing with top performing salespeople, shows that behavioral assessment has become important and it's become popular. In the past, too many people thought that a salesperson was successful if he or she looked good and sounded good. The problem was that there was no significant study or evaluation of the attitude—what goes on inside of that person. Our research now confirms that internal motivators such as the desire for financial gain or a desire to help others far outweigh looking good, sounding good, or the behavior of that salesperson in distinguishing his or her top performance.

Wright

How do you help sales professionals realize the possibilities or limits of their potential success?

Patmos

We help shape their vision, direction, and strategy around their professional purpose. In a nutshell, we help them recognize that in order to achieve success they have to be totally developed and totally focused on their objective. If they're going to reach that top echelon of performance they must recognize that development and success achievement is a science and an art. Frankly, both are needed. Each individual has to come to grips with the "behavioral facts" that pertain to him or her. We utilize benchmarking as a primary method to help professionals compare their own assessment profile to those who are at the top of the very same career, particularly in sales. Benchmarking does not compare the outputs, it compares the inputs. What we're doing is analyzing how closely their wiring matches the requirements of the position.

We have done extensive work in validated assessments as a primary mechanism to assess individuals and have them look at themselves in the behavioral mirror. They gain an understanding about what motivates them, what drives them, and what their behavioral preferences are. When individuals look internally at their own performance, behavior, and attitudes they begin to identify those characteristics that are driving them on a day-to-day basis. They possess the ability to quickly define and align what they want to do, how they want to do it and the most effective way in which they will accomplish results.

Wright

I take it you differentiate between "being successful" and saying "having success," right?

Patmos

That is absolutely true. The lines of highly successful people are almost always integrated around a purpose. We talked about that earlier. "Having success" is external. Success is something that happens to you; it's temporary at best. It's like landing that new contract or hitting your quarterly objective or meeting your sales quota for the month. "Being successful" is internal. It's a state of mind for the individual; it's a way of being. To that extent it's perpetual, never-ending, and on-going. That may seem like a small separation but when you look at the results that are achieved, there is a significant difference between those that define success internally versus those that define success externally under the category of having success.

We all have a desire to believe that our success is connected solely to us as individuals. One of the biggest lessons I have learned, at times harshly, is that you've got to recognize the cooperation, the support, and the input of others as key ingredients both in your development as well as in your success. It takes a high degree of self-reflection to recognize that our success is realized at a higher level when we align it around letting other people help us. People who may have the benefit of experience, the benefit of knowledge, and the benefit of understanding, influence us in a way that allows us to develop that internal mechanism at a higher level.

Wright

Why is it that some people seem to be "born" successful? Is that perception true?

Patmos

Let's shatter the myth that some people are "born" successful. People are born with advantages, no question about it, but the advantages are not always what we think. People tend to think of advantages as wealth, privilege, or a circle of influence. Not surprisingly, there are many examples where success has been derived out of adversity, challenge, tragedy, or trauma.

In my work, what I have found is that people who thrive with purpose, passion, and performance have very little in common as to where and what circumstances they were born into. Success requires heart and it requires soul. If you combine those, success requires a heart and soul effort, a purpose, and a passion that you can only put into something that you really desire.

When you examine why people are truly successful it's because they have gone to that level of alignment. They've done that *super thinking* about their purpose, their passion, and how they were wired. So when they say, "Here's what I want to do," "Here's what I'm going to achieve," they can align those key indexes. These people wake up every day with an enthusiasm, a passion, and a purpose that allows them to create a distinct competitive advantage in their chosen field, their chosen career, and their chosen area of expertise.

Wright

Are there some abilities or traits that are required to be successful that some people just simply don't have?

Patmos

Yes. The abilities and traits needed to be successful in sales, as an example, are very different than what it takes to be successful in customer service or to be a doctor or a nurse. Every skill set has a benefit once you define where it's appropriate. Certain people simply don't have what it takes to be successful in a given career.

Skill sets are often addressed in generalities rather than specifics. Behavioral research on the motivating factors behind why people do things suggests that if behavioral motivators and skill sets are misaligned, the chances are that there will be distinct performance and competency problems. People's dissatisfaction comes from their inability to recognize where they've been where they are and where they want to go.

Wright

On behalf of everyone who hires salespeople, what's the best way to attract and hire individuals with the greatest potential for success?

Patmos

Right off the bat we need to dispel the myth that competency is the primary method by which we should hire people. Just because somebody is competent in a skill set doesn't mean he or she is going to be successful.

The best way to attract and hire individuals with the greatest potential for success is by focusing on their behavioral patterns and the "three Cs." Assessing behaviors and motivators gives you insight into the how and why of their actions. Assessing the "three Cs" focuses on comparing and aligning the Character, Chemistry, and Culture of an individual with that of a company.

Assessing behaviors and motivators allows you to have a complete understanding of how and why someone will behave in given situations or scenarios that they may experience within the company. The objective is to understand candidates better than they understand themselves and to understand your company's environment and culture better than they understand it.

In assessing character you are comparing the honesty and integrity of the candidate with the honesty and integrity index of the company. In assessing chemistry you are comparing the intuitive fit and likeability between the candidate and the company. In assessing culture you are comparing the candidate's ability to successfully integrate into the living organism called a company.

The next thing to do is throw away the resume. What isn't being communicated in a resume is more important than what is. Resumes paint a picture of what an individual wants someone to know about him or her over a given period of time. In that resume people tell us what we want to hear. They give us the insight that they believe we want to see and it is subjective on a large scale and objective on a very small scale.

Every company or organization attracts candidates. The expectation in assessing behaviors, motivators, character, chemistry, and culture is to attract a specific group of candidates with a greater likelihood of achievement and accomplishment. Excellence attracts excellence.

Wright

Is it possible to be successful in your career and not fail in other areas of life?

Patmos

This is an area where I am a student not a teacher of the work/life balance discipline. By the way, I have to tell you that I'm not at the head of the class. When I was much younger I was certain that there was this summit to reach that enabled success in all areas of life, concurrently and consistently. What I found very quickly is that it's a rare person who has achieved a high level of success without recognizing some failures or detours in his or her career.

These represent what I like to refer to as our database for growth. Unless we learn from them continually (Perpetual Development), it makes personal and professional growth that much more difficult. If perfection were what we were all after, it would be a very boring world. I think that sometimes people say they want to be perfect at this and want to be perfect at that; it's just not a reality. You need to define the skill sets that allow you to be the best you can be at a chosen profession.

I personally will not hire anyone into our organization without some degree of demonstrated detour or lack of success; if we want to call that "failure," it's still a turning point. Detours or failures are the ways in which people learn through adversity to rise up and develop to that level of success they are either currently achieving or aspire to achieve.

You've got to be able to experience detours, distractions, and defeats in order to be successful.

Wright

What is the greatest limiting factor to success as you define it?

Patmos

Thinking you'll get there in one big step. That's just not a reality. Instead, simply take it one step at a time.

Discipline also becomes a limiting factor when people don't apply it in their personal and professional lives. "Discipline" is the ability to do what other people don't want to do, the ability to do what needs to be done when it needs to be done, and the ability to ask questions that somebody else doesn't want to ask. It is also the ability, in most cases, to ask the questions: what's the wise thing to do and/or what's the most important thing to do? When you lack that discipline it gets very hard to accomplish anything with any regularity.

Leapfrogging from here to there does happen sometimes but I call that luck rather than a plan. When that happens or when we choose to make that our primary mechanism for development, we're likely not going to be as successful as we could be.

Too many people expect comfort when they are talking about their development or success. So the third factor for limiting success may be someone's own comfort level. My advice is for people to remember that when a growth plan is developed, it shouldn't be developed with their comfort in mind. It's time for people to get out of their comfort zones if they're truly interested in achieving success.

Wright

What a great conversation, Brent. I've really appreciated your spending so much time with me answering all these questions.

Patmos

David, I appreciate that. Thank you.

About the Author

BRENT PATMOS is President and CEO of Perpetual Development, Inc. He is an accomplished author with published works including *Driven to Sell™, Success Talk™,* and *Focus on Results™*. Brent also holds the highest levels of certification as a Professional Behavioral and Values Analyst. His sales development success and his dynamic people skills have made him a sought-after consultant, speaker, and trainer. As a result, *Selling Power* magazine lists Perpetual Development among the top sales consulting companies in the United States. Brent is a professional member of the National Speakers Association and holds numerous awards and recognitions for his achievements.

Brent Patmos, CPBA, CPVA
President & CEO
Perpetual Development, Inc.
Phone: 480.812.2200
www.perpetualdevelopment.com

Chapter 11

DR. STEPHEN R. COVEY

David Wright (Wright)

We're talking today with Dr. Stephen R. Covey, cofounder and vice-chairman of Franklin Covey Company, the largest management company and leadership development organization in the world. Dr. Covey is perhaps best known as the author of *The 7 Habits of Highly Effective People* which is ranked as a number one best seller by the *New York Times*, having sold more than fourteen million copies in thirty-eight languages throughout the world. Dr. Covey is an internationally respected leadership authority, family expert, teacher, and organizational consultant. He has made teaching principle-centered living and principle-centered leadership his life's work. Dr. Covey is the recipient of the Thomas More College Medallion for Continuing Service to Humanity and has been awarded four honorary doctorate degrees. Other awards given Dr. Covey include the Sikh's 1989 International Man of Peace award, the 1994 International Entrepreneur of the Year award, *Inc.* magazine's Services Entrepreneur of the Year award, and in 1996 the National Entrepreneur of the Year Lifetime Achievement award for Entrepreneurial leadership. He has also been recognized as one of *Time* magazine's twenty-five most influential Americans and one of Sales and Marketing Management's top twenty-five power brokers. Dr. Covey earned his undergraduate degree from the University of Utah, his MBA from Harvard, and completed his doctorate at Brigham Young University. While at Brigham Young he served as assistant to the President and was also a professor of business management and organizational behavior.

Dr. Covey, welcome to *Speaking of Success!*

Dr. Stephen Covey (Covey)
Thank you.

Wright
Dr. Covey, most companies make decisions and filter them down through their organization. You, however, state that no company can succeed until individuals within it succeed. Are the goals of the company the result of the combined goals of the individuals?

Covey
Absolutely, because if people aren't on the same page, they're going to be pulling in different directions. To teach this concept, I frequently ask large audiences to close their eyes and point north, and then to keep pointing and open their eyes and they find themselves pointing all over the place. I say to them, "Tomorrow morning if you want a similar experience, ask the first ten people you meet in your organization what the purpose of your organization is and you'll find it's a very similar experience. They'll point all over the place." When people have a different sense of purpose and values, every decision that is made from then on is governed by those. There's no question that this is one of the fundamental causes of misalignment, low trust, interpersonal conflict, interdepartmental rivalry, people operating on personal agendas, and so forth.

Wright
Is that mostly a result of the inability to communicate from the top?

Covey
That's one aspect, but I think it's more fundamental. There's an inability to involve people—an unwillingness. Leaders may communicate what their mission and their strategy is, but that doesn't mean

there's any emotional connection to it. Mission statements that are rushed and then announced are soon forgotten. They become nothing more than just a bunch of platitudes on the wall that mean essentially nothing and even create a source of cynicism and a sense of hypocrisy inside the culture of an organization.

Wright

How do companies ensure survival and prosperity in these tumultuous times of technological advances, mergers, downsizing, and change?

Covey

I think that it takes a lot of high trust in a culture that has something that doesn't change—principles—at its core. There are principles that people agree upon that are valued. It gives a sense of stability. Then you have the power to adapt and be flexible when you experience these kinds of disruptive new economic models or technologies that come in and sideswipe you. You don't know how to handle them unless you have something you can depend upon. If people have not agreed to a common set of principles that guide them and a common purpose, then they get their security from the outside and they tend to freeze the structure, systems, and processes inside and they cease becoming adaptable. They don't change with the changing realities of the new marketplace out there and gradually they become obsolete.

Wright

I was interested in one portion of your book *The 7 Habits of Highly Effective People* where you talk about behaviors. How does an individual go about the process of replacing ineffective behaviors with effective ones?

Covey

I think that for most people it usually requires a crisis that humbles them to become aware of their ineffective behaviors. If there's not a crisis the tendency is to perpetuate those behaviors and not change. You don't have to wait until the marketplace creates the crisis for you. Have everyone accountable on a 360 degree basis to everyone else they interact with—with feedback either formal or informal—where they are getting data as to what's happening. They will then start to realize that the consequences of their ineffective behavior require them to be humble enough to look at that behavior and to adopt new, more effective ways of doing things. Sometimes people can be stirred up to this if you just appeal to their conscience—to their inward sense of what is right and wrong. A lot of people sometimes know inwardly they're doing wrong, but the culture doesn't necessarily discourage them from continuing that. They either need feedback from people, or they need feedback from the marketplace, or they need feedback from their conscience. Then they can begin to develop a step-by-step process of replacing old habits with new, better habits.

Wright

It's almost like saying, "Let's make all the mistakes in the laboratory before we put this thing in the air."

Covey

Right; and I also think what is necessary is a paradigm shift, which is analogous to having a correct map, say of a city or of a country. If people have an inaccurate paradigm of life, of other people, and of themselves it really doesn't make much difference what their behavior or habits or attitudes are. What they need is a correct paradigm—a correct map—that describes what's going on. For instance, in the Middle Ages they used to heal people through bloodletting. It wasn't until Samuel Weiss and Pasteur and other empirical scientists discovered the germ theory that they realized for the first time they weren't dealing with the real issue. They realized why women preferred to use midwives who washed rather than doctors who didn't wash. They gradually got a new paradigm. Once you've got a new paradigm then your behavior and your attitude flows directly from it. If you have a bad paradigm or a bad map, let's say of a city, there's no way, no matter what your behavior or your habits or your attitudes are—how positive they are—you'll never be able to find the location you're looking for. This is why I believe that to change paradigms is far more fundamental than to work on attitude and behavior.

Wright

One of your seven habits of highly effective people is to begin with the end in mind. If circumstances change and hardships or miscalculation occurs, how does one view the end with clarity?

Covey

Many people think to begin with the end in mind means that you have some fixed definition of a goal that's accomplished and if changes come about you're not going to adapt to them. Instead, the "end in mind" you begin with is that you are going to create a flexible culture of high trust so that no matter what comes along you are going to do whatever it takes to accommodate that new change or that new reality and maintain a culture of high performance and high trust. You're talking more in terms of values and overall purposes that don't change, rather than specific strategies or programs that will have to change to accommodate the changing realities in the marketplace.

Wright

In this time of mistrust between people, corporations, and nations for that matter, how do we create high levels of trust?

Covey

That's a great question and it's complicated because there are so many elements that go into the creating of a culture of trust. Obviously the most fundamental one is just to have trustworthy people. But that is not sufficient because what if the organization itself is misaligned? For instance, what if you say you value cooperation but you really reward people for internal competition? Then you have a systemic or a structure problem that creates low trust inside the culture even though the people themselves are trustworthy. This is one of the insights of Edward Demming and the work he did. That's why he said that most problems are not personal; they're systemic. They're common caused. That's why you have to work on structure, systems, and processes to make sure that they institutionalize principle-centered values. Otherwise you could have good people with bad systems and you'll get bad results.

When it comes to developing interpersonal trust between people, it is made up of many, many elements such as taking the time to listen to other people, to understand them, and to see what is important to them. What we think is important to another may only be important to us, not to another. It takes empathy. You have to make and keep promises to them. You have to treat them with kindness and courtesy. You have to be completely honest and open. You have to live up to your commitments. You can't betray them behind their back. You can't badmouth them behind their back and sweet-talk them to their face. That will send out vibes of hypocrisy and it will be detected. You have to learn to apologize when you make mistakes, to admit mistakes, and to also get feedback going in every direction as much as possible. It doesn't necessarily require formal forums; it requires trust between people that will be open with each other and give each other feedback.

Wright

My mother told me to do a lot of what you're saying now, but it seems like when I got in business I simply forgot.

Covey

Sometimes we forget, but sometimes culture doesn't nurture it. That's why I say unless you work with the institutionalizing—that means formalizing into structure, systems, and processes the values—you will not have a nurturing culture. You have to constantly work on that. This is one of the big mistakes organizations make. They think trust is simply a function of being honest. That's only one small aspect. It's an important aspect, obviously, but there are so many other elements that go into the creation of a high trust culture.

Wright

"Seek first to understand then to be understood" is another of your seven habits. Do you find that people try to communicate without really understanding what other people want?

Covey

Absolutely. The tendency is to project out of our own autobiography—our own life, our own value system—onto other people, thinking we know what they want. So we don't really listen to them. We pretend to listen, but we really don't listen from within their frame of reference. We listen from within our own frame of reference and we're really preparing our reply rather than seeking to understand. This is a very common thing. In fact very few people have had any training in seriously listening. They're trained in how to read, write, and speak, but not to listen.

Reading, writing, speaking, and listening are the four modes of communication and they represent about two-thirds to three-fourths of our waking hours. About half of that time is spent listening, but it's the one skill people have not been trained in. People have had all this training in the other forms of communication. In a large audience of

1,000 people you wouldn't have more than twenty people who have had more than two weeks of training in listening. Listening is more than a skill or a technique so that you're listening within another frame of reference. It takes tremendous courage to listen because you're at risk when you listen. You don't know what's going to happen; you're vulnerable.

Wright

Sales gurus always tell me that the number one skill in selling is listening.

Covey

Yes—listening from within the customer's frame of reference. That is so true. You can see that it takes some security to do that because you don't know what's going to happen.

Wright

With our *Speaking of Success!* talk show and book we're trying to encourage people in our audience to be better, to live better, and be more fulfilled by listening to the examples of our guests. Is there anything or anyone in your life that has made a difference for you and helped you to become a better person?

Covey

I think the most influential people in my life have been my parents. I think that what they modeled was not to make comparisons and harbor jealousy or to seek recognition. They were humble people. I remember my mother one time when we were going up in an elevator and the most prominent person in the state was in the elevator. She knew him, but she spent her time talking to the elevator operator. I was just a little kid and I was so awed by this person and I said to my mom, "Why didn't you talk to the important person?" She said, "I was. I had never met him." They were really humble, modest people who were focused on service and other people rather than on themselves. I think they were very inspiring models to me.

Wright

In almost every research paper that anyone I've ever read writes about people who influenced their lives, in the top five people, three of them are teachers. My seventh grade English teacher was the greatest teacher I ever had and influenced me to no end.

Covey

Would it be correct to say that she saw in you probably some qualities of greatness you didn't even see in yourself?

Wright

Absolutely.

Covey

That's been my general experience that the key aspect of a mentor or a teacher is someone who sees in you potential that you don't even see in yourself. They treat you accordingly and eventually you come to see it in yourself. That's my definition of leadership or influence—communicating people's worth and potential so clearly that they are inspired to see it in themselves.

Wright

Most of my teachers treated me as a student, but she treated me with much more respect than that. As a matter of fact, she called me Mr. Wright in the seventh grade. I'd never been addressed by anything but a nickname. I stood a little taller; she just made a tremendous difference. Do you think there are other characteristics that mentors seem to have in common?

Covey

I think they are first of all good examples in their own personal lives. Their personal lives and their family lives are not all messed up—they come from a base of good character. They also are usually very confident and they take the time to do what your teacher did to you—to treat you with uncommon respect and courtesy.

They also, I think, explicitly teach principles rather than practices so that rules don't take the place of human judgment. You gradually come to have faith in your own judgment in making decisions because of the affirmation of such a mentor. Good mentors care about you—you can feel the sincerity of their caring. It's like the expression, "I don't care how much you know until I know how much you care."

Wright

Most people are fascinated with the new television shows about being a survivor. What has been the greatest comeback that you've made from adversity in your career or your life?

Covey

When I was in grade school I experienced a disease in my legs. It caused me to use crutches for a while. I tried to get off them fast and get back. The disease wasn't corrected yet so I went back on crutches for another year. The disease went to the other leg and I went on for another year. It essentially took me out of my favorite thing—athletics—and it took me more into being a student. So that was kind of a life-defining experience which at the time seemed very negative, but has proven to be the basis on which I've focused my life—being more of a learner.

Wright

Principle-centered learning is basically what you do that's different from anybody I've read or listened to.

Covey

The concept is embodied in the far-eastern expression, "Give a man a fish, you feed him for the day; teach him how to fish, you feed him for a lifetime." When you teach principles that are universal and timeless, they don't belong to just any one person's religion or to a particular culture or geography. They seem to be timeless and universal like the ones we've been talking about here: trustworthiness, honesty, caring, service, growth, and development. These are universal principles. If you focus on these things then little by little people become independent of you and then they start to believe in themselves and their own judgment becomes better. You don't need as many rules. You don't need as much bureaucracy and as many controls and you can empower people.

The problem in most business operations today—and not just business but non-business—is that they're using the industrial model in an information age. Arnold Toynbee, the great historian, said, "You can pretty well summarize all of history in four words: nothing fails like success." The industrial model was based on the asset of the machine. The information model is based on the asset of the person—the knowledge worker. It's an altogether different model. But the machine model was the main asset of the twentieth century. It enabled productivity to increase fifty times. The new asset is intellectual and social capital—the qualities of people and the quality of the relationship they have with each other. Like Toynbee said, "Nothing fails like success." The industrial model does not work in an information age. It requires a focus on the new wealth, not capital and material things.

A good illustration that demonstrates how much we were into the industrial model, and still are, is to notice where people are on the balance sheet. They're not found there. Machines are found there. Machines become investments. People are on the profit and loss statement and people are expenses. Think of that—if that isn't blood-letting.

Wright

It sure is.

When you consider the choices you've made down through the years, has faith played an important role in your life?

Covey

It has played an extremely important role. I believe deeply that we should put principles at the center of our lives, but I believe that God is the source of those principles. I did not invent them. I get credit sometimes for some of the Seven Habits material and some of the other things I've done, but it's really all based on principles that have been given by God to all of His children from the beginning of time. You'll find that you can teach these same principles from the sacred texts and the wisdom literature of almost any tradition. I think the ultimate source of that is God and that is one thing you can absolutely depend upon—in God we trust.

Wright

If you could have a platform and tell our audience something you feel would help them or encourage them, what would you say?

Covey

I think I would say to put God at the center of your life and then prioritize your family. No one on their deathbed ever wished they spent more time at the office.

Wright

That's right. We have come down to the end of our program and I know you're a busy person, but I could talk with you all day Dr. Covey.

Covey

It's good to talk with you as well and to be a part of this program. It looks like an excellent one that you've got going on here.

Wright

Thank you.

We have been talking today with Dr. Stephen R. Covey, co-founder and vice-chairman of Franklin Covey Company. He's also the author of *The 7 Habits of Highly Effective People,* which has been ranked as a number one bestseller by the *New York Times,* selling more than fourteen million copies in thirty-eight languages.

Dr. Covey, thank you so much for being with us today on *Speaking of Success!*

Covey

Thank you for the honor of participating.

About The Author

Stephen R. Covey was recognized in 1996 as one of Time magazine's twenty-five most influential Americans and one of Sales and Marketing Management's top twenty-five power brokers. Dr. Covey is the author of several acclaimed books, including the international bestseller, The 7 Habits of Highly Effective People. It has sold more than fifteen million copies in thirty-eight languages throughout the world. Other bestsellers authored by Dr. Covey include First Things First, Principle-Centered Leadership (with sales exceeding one million), and The 7 Habits of Highly Effective Families.

Dr. Covey's newest book, The 8th Habit: From Effectiveness to Greatness, which was released in November 2004, rose to the top of several bestseller lists, including New York Times, Wall Street Journal, USA Today, Money, Business Week, and Amazon.com and Barnes & Noble. The 8th Habit . . . has sold more than 360,000 copies.

Dr. Covey earned his undergraduate degree from the University of Utah, his MBA from Harvard, and completed his doctorate at Brigham Young University. While at Brigham Young University, he served as assistant to the President and was also a professor of business management and organizational behavior. He received the National Fatherhood Award in 2003, which, as the father of nine and grandfather of forty-four, he says is the most meaningful award he has ever received.

Dr. Covey currently serves on the board of directors for the Points of Light Foundation. Based in Washington, D.C., the Foundation, through its partnership with the Volunteer Center National Network, engages and mobilizes millions of volunteers from all walks of life—businesses, nonprofits, faith-based organizations, low-income communities, families, youth, and older adults—to help solve serious social problems in thousands of communities.

Dr. Stephen R. Covey
www.stephencovey.com

Chapter 12

GORDON GRAHAM

THE INTERVIEW

David Wright (Wright)

Today we're talking with Gordon Graham. Gordon is one of the nation's most sought-after and well-respected change agents in the areas of labor/management and corrections. His background, communication skills, and total commitment to the change process sets him apart from the myriad of speakers and trainers in today's world. Gordon is a product of what he shares with his audiences: "Change is possible, but it's a do-it-yourself project. We provide new techniques for people who are seeking change."

Gordon, welcome to *Speaking of Success.*

To begin with, what separates Gordon Graham from the myriad of speakers on change?

Gordon Graham (Graham)

Dealing with a rapidly changing world is critical today, and change management is a hot topic. Most of the speakers, consultants, and trainers working in the area of change are really speaking about the same thing; there's not much new material out there when it comes to motivating people and managing change. Where I differ from other speakers is in background and style.

My style is just a bit different from most, and maybe sometimes a little bit easier to connect with because it comes directly from experience and allows people to discover *for themselves* where they might be stuck, blocked, or trapped.

Most of the speakers out there come from an academically solid knowledge base that lends tremendous value and credibility to their presentations. I have tremendous respect for that background, academic training, and knowledge. I think the thing that separates me from most speakers is that every single thing I teach is based strictly on life experience. Don't get me wrong, the material has academic validity, but what I teach changed my own life in very dramatic ways.

I'm not trying to dictate or tell people what they should or shouldn't do when I teach or present information. My approach to change is the self-discovery process. I translate sometimes very complicated information into practical terms, and people make a choice whether or not to implement that information into their lives. I ask them to start with themselves and test the information first. Once people see it work in their personal lives and in the lives of their families, they become excited about implementing the concepts in the workplace.

Wright

You mention that this material changed your life in dramatic ways. Would you describe for our readers your own personal transformation? How does a person go from cracking safes to become an internationally known expert on change?

Graham

Well, clearly I needed to change careers. I didn't experience too much success cracking safes since I kept getting caught and winding up in prison. And I knew I didn't want to stay there for the rest of my life, but I had no idea where to even begin to change.

At one point I was released from a prison they liked so much that they named it twice—a place called Walla Walla. I was trying to revive my professional boxing career and a couple of friends of mine—a fight promoter and another person—encouraged me to go to this seminar that a guy was teaching at a resort in Port Ludlow, Washington.

At that time in my life I had no idea what a seminar was. This was during the 1970s and a time of "T-groups" in which the learners use feedback, problem-solving, and role-play to gain insights into themselves, others, and groups. I thought a seminar was one of those touchy-feely kinds of activities where you go out in the country and cry, hug each other, throw-up, and go back to work. I said, "I don't need no damn seminar; what I need is some money!"

They convinced me that it wasn't that kind of thing. They set up a meeting with the guy who taught the seminar, Lou Tice. Louis was a high school football coach and athletic director. He made the study of human behavior his field. After listening to Louis for an afternoon I got interested in attending, so they told me they would pay my way if I went through it. So my first wife, Jane, and I spent three and a half days at a seminar called "Achieving Your Potential." When Lou started teaching I looked around and thought to myself, "What am I doing here?" The seminar was filled with business leaders and professional athletes, and me—a former safe-cracker.

But as Louis continued to teach I felt like I was in a dark room and I couldn't see. Then someone started opening the blinds and at the end of those three and a half days I started to discover what was keeping me stuck the whole time.

My partner, David Lewis, from East Palo Alto, former Black Gorilla gang leader and ex-offender, has a non-profit agency called "Free at Last." Well, I came out of that seminar three and a half days later free at last. I knew what I hadn't known before. I'm sure counselors and psychologists had told me countless times, but I wasn't ready to hear it or see it—you don't know what you don't know.

The first step to change is awareness. I came out of that seminar with a new awareness of how to take control of my life and how to take accountability for my life. A lot of it was common sense, but in the world I came from, common sense isn't always that common.

I think that awareness is the first step, but if there isn't some support or nourishment combined with ongoing application, people fall back into the same old behavior and thinking patterns. Change takes tenacity, resiliency, and a support system to help sustain the changes long enough for them to become internalized as a part of who we really are.

Wright

Why do you believe that you can impact the lives of inmates in prison, and how do you actually reach them to get them to consider change?

Graham

Many people in mainstream society look at our inmate population as different than we are, and so they treat them differently—often they are treated as "less than" the rest of us. When I work with men and women in prison I see them no differently than I see myself. They are just like I was before I started to use these concepts to change the way I think. I understand that when I was sitting in their position in those same denim blues, I thought just like they think.

Inmates in prison recognize that I have tremendous empathy. I understand where they are coming from. I recognize there are certainly some people in prison who have to stay in prison. I mean, there are some dangerous people who need to be there. I also believe that many inmates, like anybody else, really want to change but don't know how; not all of them of course, but as a general statement many inmates are just like you and me. They are stuck in thinking traps that put them in a situation that is difficult to change. Correctional institutions are not really conducive to positive change. Unfortunately, prisons do not change people or their thinking patterns for the better. Instead, many people go into prison with a sprained ankle and come out with a broken leg.

Wright

So how did you get into this business?

Graham

Have you ever read a book that you couldn't wait to share with someone you love? Or have you ever seen a movie and told your friends they need to go see that movie? Well, when I came out of that seminar my first thought was, "I've got to get this information back into prisons where there are a lot of people just like me who want to change and don't know how."

Now, all of these years later, my *Breaking Barriers* program is in prisons all over the United States and other parts of the world. *Breaking Barriers* reaches and influences the inmate population better than any cognitive skills program used in prisons today. My success in that arena led to opportunities in the business world as well.

All of this really started with that one personally enlightening experience with Lou Tice and the Pacific Institute.

Wright

What is your major focus when working with business and industry?

Graham

My objective is to create awareness for people that the culture you work in—the culture you live in—drives your performance. People perform better and grow more in cultures that promote dignity, respect, and creativity. We can't motivate people long-term using fear and coercion. To really grow into our potential, we need to feel valued and connected to the goals of the organization.

My message to union/management groups of any kind, whether it is industry, military, corrections, or education is the same. When organizations stay stuck in old ways of power versus rights, they do not compete as effectively in today's world. Staying stuck in old ruts is easier than working to change.

A friend of mine was talking about a stretch of dirt road in Missouri where his father grew up as a boy. In the rainy season that stretch of road would get very muddy. The cars driving over that thirty-mile stretch of road would dig deep ruts in the road. As you entered that stretch of road there was a conspicuous sign beside the road that said, "Choose your rut carefully; you'll be in it for the next 30 miles."

But there should be a sign beside our lives that says the same thing: "Choose your rut carefully; you'll be in it for the next thirty years." The problem with being in a rut is that you don't know you are in it. It gradually and incrementally becomes normal, accepted behavior. My approach is to try to get people to recognize *for themselves* that change is possible, you are accountable for your own life, you are accountable for your part in your organization, and if things aren't working for you, you need to do something to change it.

There really isn't any magic in what I do, but I think the example I demonstrate in my own life makes an impact on people. My background is quite different than your ordinary motivational speaker or change management professional. Every time I speak I am a living example of the impact of these concepts. People like the feeling that if someone with my background can change, so can they.

Wright

You mentioned the impact a culture has on performance. Will you tell us more about that?

Graham

Culture is one of the things we deal with on a continuous basis in the trainings we conduct for organizations. Much of our work is based on research by John Kotter and James Heskett from the Harvard Business School. In eleven years of research, Dr. Kotter and Dr. Heskett demonstrated that high performing cultures focus on the growth of leadership and engagement of people. They put 207 firms into two categories: those with defensive cultures and those with constructive cultures. In every bottom-line category, the organizations with a constructive culture dramatically outperformed the defensive cultures.

When a young man or woman comes out of college or school, he or she works like heck to get a job, and once that job is obtained the culture of that office or industrial plant will gradually and incrementally shape the way the individual perceives the business and the people in it. If the culture is constructive, people will learn creativity, growth, and productivity. If the culture is defensive, they'll end up trading time for money and spend a lot of time and energy finding ways to get even with the people they supposedly work for.

Gordon Graham and Company and The Pacific Institute are organizations that are committed to educating people about the impact of culture on people and the critical nature of creating cultures that are positive and sustained.

Our families have a culture, our communities have a culture, our schools have a culture, and prisons have a culture. In each case, the type of culture we create will without a doubt dictate our performance.

When I first went to prison as a young man of eighteen or nineteen years, I was a pretty tough kid. I was busted in a little town in Washington for first degree forgery, a felony. I was sent to prison for fifteen months, and with good behavior I would have been out in ten months. I went into prison for the first time, thinking like a scared young man. Then I adjusted to the culture, and six years later I came out of that prison thinking like a convict. It was a slow and subtle transformation of the way that I thought. And it turned a ten-month sentence into six years—and I carried that thought pattern into the next dozen years after that.

If an offender or inmate can learn to handle that culture more effectively, then perhaps he or she can maintain some kind of positive outlook despite the prison experience. It takes a lot of tenacity and a lot of desire, but it can be done.

Wright

Can one individual, in your opinion, truly make a difference?

Graham

Yes, and it takes tremendous courage, tenacity, and resiliency. I've experienced successes where a single plant manager and a union chair each changed his or her own thinking patterns and as a result they changed an industrial plant from a defensive culture to a constructive culture. One particular plant was close to the worst plant in the division and transformed itself through this education to become the number one plant in that division.

I also believe that an individual taking on a culture must be doing it for the right reasons. People can read insincerity and get very turned off by people who are doing it for the wrong reasons. If they are working toward personal glory and personal reward, it goes against everything we teach about great leadership. Rewards are important, but people who do this for the right reasons aim to create a culture where people are treated fairly, where people have equal access to opportunities, and where people are honest. Leaders like that have a tremendous impact on the culture. I would like to think that my company provides people with the tools to create and sustain that kind of culture.

One person can also make a difference in a community. Years ago, East Palo Alto was dubbed the Murder Capital of the United States. David Lewis, a former consumer of correctional services (I mentioned him earlier), used the concepts in our education to turn his own life around. He and the mayor of East Palo Alto, Sharifa Wilson, teamed up to impact the culture of their community. They involved law-enforcement officers, ex-offenders, social service agencies, and businesses to transform East Palo Alto into a safe, constructive community. The result was they reduced violence by 86 percent and David won the California Peace Prize. It is possible for one person to make an impact, but again, it takes courage, audacity, and the tools to do it.

Wright

How do you measure your success? And how should others measure theirs?

Graham

Success is an interesting thing and it differs based on the environment. Profit-making organizations measure success with bottom-line results. Unions measure success by keeping jobs in their communities and in this country. Membership numbers are also an indicator of success for a union. Individuals measure success in many different ways, some of which can lead to healthy, happy lifestyles and some can lead to misery and frustration. Parents often measure their success by raising healthy, productive children.

For me, my success comes from making a positive difference in the lives of others and making an impact on the world. I intend to devote my life to impacting others in a positive way.

People often define success for others the way they define it for themselves. For example, we have a very small office here in Bellevue, Washington, and each of us defines success differently, even though we are working toward the same end result. Success should come from enjoying what you're doing and being rewarded equitably for what you do, and then having opportunities to better yourself or your situation.

Unfortunately, many people in our society are playing without all of the tools, and are not playing on a level playing field. I know first-hand that many of our fellow citizens do not have equal access to opportunities. My personalized license plate says "nthgame" (in the game). I try to keep people focused on playing the hand they are dealt. I think to be successful you've got to be in the game, whatever the game is for you in your life.

Wright

What is the message that you want people to take away from your seminars or speeches?

Graham

I use entertainment and humor to get my message across. Above all else, I want people to walk away from my seminars recognizing that they can make a difference, that they are either a part of the problem or part of the solution, that each of us is accountable for our own decisions, and that there are no "have to's" in life. There are always choices. Sometimes the choices aren't too good; but there are always choices.

I stress to people that the way we think becomes a habit, just like anything else. If you change the way you think, you will change the way you act. If we continue to face our problems the same way, with the same thinking patterns, we continue to get the same results. It is critical to change our approach to the challenges we face in our lives.

Let me use an example from my own background. The last time I was sent to prison I was shot in a burglary set-up. I didn't know how bad I was hit, so I told my partner "Man, you drive." My partner had grown up in prison, so he couldn't drive a stick-shift automobile. So the cops came swooping in and trapped us.

They had been dealing with me for years. One of them said, "There's been some shooting up here."

"I don't know nothing about any shooting," I replied, as I'm bleeding from the legs. To make a long story short, they found a pistol in the car and sent us back to prison for five years on a charge of felons in possession of a firearm. Guess where I placed the blame? I blamed my partner for not being able to drive a stick-shift automobile. The time before that, I had a bad lawyer. The time before that, I had a bad judge. And I can remember before that blaming society—"they" and "them out there."

I recognized thirty-five years ago that I am accountable. If I have a bad day, it's my fault. And I just don't choose to have bad days. I may have a bad fifteen minutes or so, but I don't choose to have bad days. It is just not the way that I want to think. It isn't pie in the sky; it is recognizing that I am fully accountable for how and what I think about, and that the way I think controls the way I act.

Wright

What legacy will you leave this world and who will carry on your message?

Graham

I would like to think that the world is just a wee bit better because I was here, and I'd like to leave it with the feeling that I was able to make a positive difference. And I hope to maximize the gifts I was blessed with, while leaving the world when I'm fully maxed out. I don't want to leave anything on the table—I want to use it all up.

I've had all kinds of experiences in my life. Some positive and some negative. And I've had about every experience a person can imagine, so when I leave I want to feel satisfied that I've given this world my all.

I like to think of myself as planting the seeds of positive change. To use an analogy that I like—if you cut an apple in half, anybody can count the seeds in an apple; but no one can count the apples in a seed. Someone planted a seed in me over thirty-five years ago. In turn, I've had the opportunity to plant many, many seeds over the years. The seed needs to be planted on fertile ground. It needs nurturing with support and follow-through. But none of us ever knows where and when that seed might take root. I keep that in mind with everything that I do.

I also hope that I've paved the way for others to carry on this work. David Lewis is committed to the mission of changing lives. I also have an associate in my office, Cathy Crosslin, who has worked with me for about twelve years. She is a tremendous presenter and one of the best facilitators I've ever been around. Cat is a great advocate of the change process and she can do just about everything I can do. And she didn't have to spend time in prison to learn it! Her background in athletics and education bring a different perspective to the curriculum, and she will continue to make an impact in the world.

Wright

Why should the average citizen be concerned about our prison population?

Graham

Our country finds itself in a situation with the prison system that is not manageable long-term. We have 750,000 men and women each year coming out of the prison system and going back into communities where opportunities are scarce and resources are slim.

We have a large, large number of people locked up who could be managed in a more effective and humane manner that would lead to greater success in the transition out of prison. But there is a perception in the business of corrections that it is too costly to provide education, training, and cognitive skills processes to the incarcerated. I hope that we are on the cusp of change in this area.

There are tremendous alternatives we could implement, but one of the primary challenges is dealing with the politics of providing services to the incarcerated. I'm not saying anything negative about politicians, but to get elected, a politician usually needs to take a "tough on crime" platform. We do have some very dangerous people who should be locked up for life. But we also have a lot of people locked up for long periods of time who could be managed in a more effective way with better long-term results, ultimately impacting recidivism in the process. If we are truly concerned about public safety, then we need to do a much better job of handling the re-entry process for those men and women coming back into our communities. Tough on crime does not always translate into public safety.

I'm an advocate for public safety. I have a whole bunch of grandchildren and I want them to be safe, and I want my communities to be safe. I would like for the system to do the best job possible to provide re-entry and transitional services that actually accomplish this goal.

Wright

Today we have been talking with Gordon Graham. As we have found, he offers readers an opportunity to experience change through a very unique perspective. His ability to connect with diverse groups is a rare gift. His work in prisons and union/management environments has made a dramatic impact on the lives of thousands of individuals. You can read more about Gordon in his autobiographies: *The One Eyed Man is King* and *Change is an Inside Job.* To order, please visit www.ggco.com.

Gordon, thank you so much for being with us today on *Speaking of Success.*

Graham

Thank you, it has been a pleasure.

About the Author

The founder of his own company, Gordon Graham provides educational materials and presents live seminars to organizations across the United States and Canada. Through his renowned training series, Gordon has been facilitating change for individuals and organizations for more than thirty years. Graham is one of the most sought-after and well respected change agents in the areas of labor management and corrections. His background, communication skills, and total commitment to the change process set him apart from the myriad of speakers and trainers in today's world. Graham's clients report improvements in the areas of communication, product quality, productivity, and employee involvement. "Gordon's delivery, combined with a humorous and thought-provoking presentation, establishes awareness that it's never too late for a new beginning," said Paul Loberg of Eagle Crest Properties. Graham's programs have been implemented successfully in a variety of settings, and his approach reaches people from all backgrounds. Clients include corporate executives, union/management personnel, state and federal agencies, at-risk youth, and prison inmates.

Gordon Graham
Gordon Graham & Company
P.O. Box 3927
Bellevue, WA 98009
Phone: 425.637.9992
Fax: 425.637.0144
E-mail: customerservice@ggco.com
www.ggco.com

Chapter 13

THE INTERVIEW

David Wright (Wright)

Today we are talking with Daniel Abramson, CTS, president and founder of StaffDynamics. He has been focused on workforce performance strategies and raising the bar for over twenty-five years. Prior to StaffDynamics, Daniel was president of an international staffing firm with over 120 offices. Under his leadership revenues nearly tripled and profits increased almost nine-fold, making him uniquely qualified to guide both individuals and corporations in exceeding their operational and financial objectives. Daniel earned his bachelor's degree in Marketing and has MBA credits. He is a certified instructor of Xerox Professional Selling Skills and DISC Personality Assessments. He has also completed the Dale Carnegie program and is a member of the National Speakers Association and the National Association of Training and Development. Daniel is also author of Secrets of Hiring Top Talent, available on Amazon.com. He lives in the Washington, D.C., area with his wife, two daughters, and a bevy of pets.

Daniel, welcome to *Speaking of Success.*
So what is it exactly that you do?

Daniel Abramson (Abramson)

I help companies increase revenues and decrease costs by focusing on talent, strategy, and execution. I find that good companies start with great people. I also find that many companies don't do a good job hiring people. They don't have a solid strategy as far as what they want to achieve, and the biggest issue that many companies face today is poor execution and accountability. Firms must hold people accountable to make sure they raise the bar and get the job done.

Wright

What makes you different from other speakers and consultants?

Abramson

That's a great question.

As you know, there are a lot of great speakers and consultants out there. My "differentiator" is that I've worked both sides of the desk. Not only have I been a consultant, speaker, and coach—as I am now—but I've been involved in running a large corporation and I know what it's like to hire good people, run offices, meet deadlines, meet payroll, manage expenses, and increase the bottom line.

The company I ran was a subsidiary of a large public corporation, so my team and I were required to deliver performance, profitability, and growth on a quarterly basis. Having done that with some success, and having been a presenter and trainer in one capacity or another for most of my professional career, I think I have a unique handle on the theory and the practical reality of what it's like to take a vision and put it into practice on a day-to-day basis.

Wright

How did you get into the speaking and consulting industry?

Abramson

In 2001, I had been with an international staffing company for almost sixteen years, running my own office in Rhode Island for the first six. From my base as a franchisee, I was promoted to President and CEO of this firm in New York where I made a significant contribution to revenues and profits during the next ten years.

I then decided I'd had enough of the corporate life, and to cash out my options, and do something on my own. This was just a few months before the horrible events in September 2001. Like most of us, I had no idea at the time that the entire planet would be so impacted by 9/11. Faced with the sweeping changes that affected us all after 9/11, I determined to reengineer myself and take a different path.

My business model is to use my speaking skills as a vehicle for generating consulting assignments. I speak in front of large organizations, always focusing on value rather than just entertainment, so the people who participate can take something of value away.

After most of those events, people come up to me, hand me their business cards, and ask me to call them. Those follow-up calls have in turn created many different business opportunities—most of which fall under the umbrella of consulting, speaking, and coaching.

I believe that one should deliver value first by giving valuable insights and techniques to people for free so that they can develop a focused image of how you can help them or their firms improve. By doing that, and by keeping myself out in the public eye, the rest seems to take care of itself.

So my business strategy, even today, is to use my speaking as a vehicle to get people's minds going, which in turn generates new business.

Wright

What do you think is the "special sauce" that makes companies successful?

Abramson

Great companies today put their people first, not only financially, but also by letting them know that how valuable they are to the company. These great companies give their employees opportunities to grow—both personally and professionally.

One strong gauge of companies that are doing a great job is low turnover. When companies start to fail, one of the first things you'll notice is a dramatic increase in turnover—accompanied by low morale. In these failing companies the energy is gone, there's no passion, and most employees dread coming to work. While this insight is pretty basic, it's amazing how many companies just don't "get" it. To make matters worse, they react to poor performance by developing a "bunker" mentality and becoming punitive. As the classic sign on the manager's door reads, "The beatings will continue until morale improves."

Wright

In a service-based industry, why are "soft skills" more important than technical skills?

Abramson

It's a sad fact that most companies today hire for skills and fire for personality. That is, they focus more on what a new hire *has done* than on what he or she *will do*. While the skill match may look like a good one at the time of the hire, soft-skill factors kick in (or, just as likely, fail to do so) over time and those companies are forced to terminate a good number of those hires because of personality issues.

When assessing soft skills—behavior, attitude, work ethic, and compatibility—you can't make the determination you need by reviewing a person's resume. And yet these four character traits I call the "soft skills" are the glue that holds people together, builds teams and provides lasting value to companies.

Given what I've seen in the staffing industry and as an independent consultant, I have come to believe that, in general, companies have to do a much better job interviewing and understanding the soft skills of the candidates they hire to make sure that chemistry and fit are both compatible and will nurture a positive contribution.

Wright

Back in the early '70s I learned what I still believe to be true. I subscribe to the theory that everything can be defined by its characteristics. So would you tell me what some of the success traits in hiring for today's workforce are?

Abramson

When you look at a person's resume, the soft skills of behavior—attitude, work ethic, and passion in the belly—are well-hidden under the accepted norms of resume writing. So asking questions about what a candidate has done in the past is important. Companies today have to do a much better job interviewing behaviorally rather than asking questions like, "Tell me where you want to be four or five years from now." This means probing what makes a candidate tick, finding out if and/or how he or she gains satisfaction from the work environment, posing hypotheticals and listening carefully to how the candidate reacts to them, observing the candidate's eye contact and behavior in person and on the phone, viewing and discussing work samples, and observing how the candidate interacts in a group, among other things, to get a total picture of how the candidate is put together and how he or she might fit in with your team.

Most people stay in a company today about eighteen months or two years. Back in the '80s it was very common for people to come out of high school or college and stay in the same job for eighteen to twenty years. We remember the era when people would stay at a company for a long time, retire, and receive a gold watch or a pen. Unfortunately, those days are gone and voluntary turnover in our country is running about 20 percent per year.

Today people just don't stay put for long, so it's really important to interview behaviorally, to ask those "what-if" questions, and to focus on motivators to determine what's important to the candidate. And just to add a little spice to the interviewing pie, we have the largest number of generations in the workforce in history: Generation X, Generation Y, and the Baby Boomers. What motivates and why each of these groups come to work is extensively different, which makes behavioral interviewing even more critical.

The other thing that is very important is that many companies don't let staff members and potential co-workers participate in the interviewing process. I think one of the best ways to uncover behavior, attitude, work ethic, and fit is to have another people—including peers—interview the candidate. The boss doesn't always get a good read on a new person coming in for an interview—too much is at stake and the candidate is on his or her best behavior.

Whether we realize it or not, the success of every business in the twenty-first century is driven by service. Even if we manufacture basic industrial products, we compete with rest of the world on service, availability, and price—and availability is another form of service, as is creative pricing. Even if our primary sales channel is a Web site, it is our people who provide that web of service that engenders customer satisfaction and loyalty and slows our businesses to thrive. Therefore the intellectual capital of every business that thrives today is based on "people"—on knowledge workers. This is a very different concept than the industrial model that viewed people as cogs in a machine, and it is (or it ought to be) a great source of inspiration for our age.

What makes people work well together are soft skills. And soft skills are the key ingredients of the "special sauce" that draws great companies together.

Wright

In reading some of the things you do I read things like communication, flexibility, and being proactive and team oriented. Would you speak to some of those issues?

Abramson

Being pro-active, being team-oriented, being competitive, and being a person who wants to get the job done is not something I invented—it is today's business mantra for the individual contributor. It is also almost as important as a person who can work with and through people. In today's business world, people do business with people they trust, who are friendly and engaging and who don't waste each other's time. You can't teach these skills. A person is friendly, engaging, and time-sensitive or he or she is not.

The last thing I tell companies during my seminars and consulting engagements is to hire people who are fun to be with. Business today can sometimes be intense and chaotic; competition can be fierce and deadlines crushing. In today's lean organizations, people are required to wear a lot of hats, juggle balls, and keep the plates spinning, so you have to enjoy your work and like your coworkers. You have to make it fun. You have to hire people who can thrive on chaos and who don't take themselves too seriously.

Wright

Every time I pick up the paper now I read articles where the headlines don't read integrity but the whole article does. What do you think about integrity in the workforce today?

Abramson

I think those are critical words—integrity and character are the backbone of any company employee. We all talk about that, but character and integrity are truly the most important factors in any person's makeup. These are not qualities you develop in college or high school; they are developed within you during your upbringing. You either have them or you don't. And they're impossible to gauge from a resume alone.

One my favorite questions that I like to ask candidates to probe character and integrity is, "Give me an example of a time where you had to break or stretch the rules in order to get something done." I like that question because I don't mind if a person works the edges but I have a big problem if people find it acceptable to break the rules or do something that borders on being dishonest regarding the job. So I'm listening for how far he or she pushed the envelope and whether the decision to stray from the straight and narrow was an easy or difficult one.

Wright

One of the things I remember reading about you was the trait of empathy. You talk about respect of differences. Will you speak to that issue?

Abramson

Sure. As you mentioned, empathy is being able to walk in someone else's shoes. In a service-based business culture where we're dealing with customers all the time, we have to be able to listen and hear very well. We have to be able to empathize with that customer. We have to be able to make good decisions—ones that will satisfy the customer without undermining the integrity of the product or company. Empathy is a very important part of this.

Here's another undervalued but very important trait: business intuition. Intuition in business is the ability to make good decisions with incomplete information. When I hire, I'm looking for people who, if I give them A and B, can make it to C and D by themselves without constant handholding. We talked before about the secret sauce of good companies. Most companies today are small companies with fifty employees or less, so everyone has to be a knowledge worker. And there's never enough information, so strong intuitive skills are very important.

Wright

In your opinion, what companies really "get it" regarding sales, customer service, and wowing the customer?

Abramson

I travel a hundred thousand miles a year crisscrossing the country speaking and consulting with companies. One of the most impressive companies I see on a continuous basis is Southwest Airlines. No matter who you speak with or who you call, Southwest Airlines employees are very friendly, very engaging, and always have a get-it-done attitude.

Marriott Hotels is another great example of a company that "gets it." When you check in, the desk clerks are very efficient and very helpful.

Another company I absolutely enjoy is Starbucks. Starbucks hires lots of different people of different ages, some funky, and some conservative; but when you go into a Starbucks, the place is clean, you always have a terrific experience, people are friendly, and the product is fresh.

Another company that clearly "gets it" is Chick-fil-A, which was started by Truett Cathy. When you go to any one of those restaurants everyone is polite, the product is terrific, and the place is immaculate.

These companies "get it" because they provide great products, a great service, which means their people are well-trained, and they give you that *wow!* experience.

So much today is based on what people think about the product or service they buy. A statistic I like is that when a person has a good experience with a product or service, that person will tell eight other people. But when a person has a bad experience with a product or service, he or she will tell sixteen people. That's a terrible cost. And it's all because of something the company failed to execute properly in the areas of hiring, training, or systems and procedures.

The bottom line is this: customers today are very fussy and they have high demands regarding quality. They want good service. Period!

I'll give you an example of a company that doesn't get it. One of the major airlines uses a call center over in Indonesia and India. It is very difficult to work with some of these offshore call centers because even though a lot of those people do speak English, they just don't "get it" as far as connecting with the customer. If you contact a Southwest Airlines call center, on the other hand, it is located in the United States, the phone is answered on the second ring, the people are friendly and engaging—they "get it."

People do business with people they like, trust, and who are friendly and engaging.

Wright

I interviewed Truett Cathy, founder of Chick-fil-A. We had a long conversation and during that conversation the statistics came up. He says he loses about $500 million a year in sales simply because he will not open on Sunday. He says it's just wrong. You can hardly argue with that.

Abramson

That's a perfect example of a gentleman who philosophically does what he believes. Chick-fil-A is in a lot of mall locations and when you go into the mall on Sunday, they're closed. But it's interesting how Chick-fil-A has turned that positive into a negative—they have a big sign in their restaurant that says, "Interested in having Sundays off? Apply Monday through Saturday for a great career!"

Wright

They also pay a lot of children's way through college, something that no one knows about.

Abramson

True. Truett Cathy started with one Chick-fil-A in Atlanta and no college education. When you go into a Chick-fil-A the people are friendly and they "get it." They also have a great tasting product.

Wright

I know that you wrote a book titled, *Secrets of Hiring Top Talent.* I'm curious—what are the secrets?

Abramson

The secrets include some of the things we have talked about. It's really not that complicated—you have to hire good people and you have to interview each person more than one time. I think many more companies than you might realize make the fatal mistake of interviewing and then hiring someone immediately after that first interview. The difficulty with that method is candidates can do a Google search for the top ten interview questions and become professional interviewees. You have to dig down and get inside the person to see what motivates him or her regarding the soft skills of behavior, attitude, and work ethic. That takes time, and more than one shapshot of what makes that person tick.

The other big secret is making sure that other associates in your company interview job candidates to get buy-in. A big mistake companies make is to hire someone, then introduce the new person into the company, and there's no buy-in with the staff. Staff members re-sent that. They do better when they are involved in the decision-making process. When they're not, morale suffers, and turnover starts to increase. Your existing staff members are also less likely to make the new-hire feel welcome under those circumstances.

Wright

We've talked a lot about soft skills and I read in your bio that you are certified in the DISC Personality Assessment. I'm very fascinated by that tool. Obviously you believe in personality assessments as part of the hiring process. Will you tell our readers a little bit more about this?

Abramson

I mentioned today that we're all in a service-based business where chemistry, fit, and corporate compatibility are the most critical components of the hiring process. Yet, unfortunately, when we interview someone we can easily get fooled. We rely on our gut based on how a person talks or how a person looks or where a person went to high school or college and we make mistakes.

One of the tools I recommend is a personality assessment. There are several of them that have been around long enough to have developed proven track records. The DISC survey is the one I like the best. It was developed almost fifty years ago, and it measures four different personality traits:

- D stands for dominance
- I stands for interaction or people skills
- S stands for steadiness
- C stands for compliance—will you comply, will you do what you're told?

I like to refer to this as an instrument rather than a test because a test is something you can pass or fail and a Personality Assessment is just a tool—a snapshot—of one's personality. The nice thing about this instrument is that it measures personality in two different environments. One is how you behave at work and the second is how you behave under stress or pressure, which reveals the true self. The DISC thus measures those four traits in a work environment as well as away from work.

What I teach companies to look for is consistency both on the court and off the court as opposed to a Dr. Jekyll and Mr. Hyde who acts one way at work and another way away from work. Again, most companies are small, everyone has to get along, and everyone is a knowledge worker.

I recommend that you benchmark the most successful salespeople, accounting people, and customer service people so that you know behaviorally what the successful profile looks like for each group. This way, when you're bringing a prospective salesperson in, for example, you have a benchmark to measure against to make sure that candidate's the soft skills are compatible with maximum performance in your organization.

If you are looking for a salesperson, you will want the skill traits of people who shore high on dominance or assertiveness and who also have good people skills. They would rank high in the D and the I sections of the DISC assessment. If you are looking for an accountant or a back-office operations person, you want someone who is steady, goes with the program, enforces the rules, and makes sure everything is buttoned up (i.e., someone who makes sure all the details and the processes are absolutely in place).

These are very different kinds of personality traits, each with its own very important contributions to make. In service-based economy, I believe the personality assessment tool is a very important step in the interview process.

Many people ask how much these tools cost. The investment is only $75 and $100 per person, based on volume. I believe that's fairly inexpensive insurance compared to the cost of a bad hire. As an example, if you hire someone and that person leaves for whatever reason, that bad hire can cost three to five times his or her salary. If you're hiring a $60,000 person, that can be a $180,000 mistake as it relates to the morale of your staff, bad customer service with your clients, re-hiring and training, missed deadlines, lost sales, etc.

What we've been talking about here is one of the secrets of hiring top talent. The secrets include multiple interviews—having your staff or other associates in the company interview the prospective employee—and adding in the personality assessment as an acid test to make sure the chemistry is a good fit and the personality is compatible with the job for which you're hiring.

Wright

Tell me a little bit about how you go about coaching a company and its leaders. Before our interview is over I'd like to know what do you generally find are the obstacles?

Abramson

I just came back yesterday from Florida with a client I secured as a result of the CEO attending my speaking seminar. This company has thirty-five people, grosses about $140 million, and is growing rapidly.

The first thing I do in a coaching assignment is talk with the president about goals and objectives and about the outcomes he would like to see. I asked him if he had a magic wand, what three things would he like to see changed or improved? Many presidents seem to have trouble answering this simple question.

The second thing I do is talk with the key managers in the company one-on-one. One of the most striking things that I find is the discrepancy between what the president perceives is going on and what the issues are and the reality of what the managers think. I also talk with some of the department heads one level down.

In talking with all of these people, I can form a pretty good picture, as far as perceptions, realities, and issues go. The thing that is startling to me is how different these perceptions and realities often are.

The next thing I'll do is conduct a DISC personality assessment on these groups because I want to see behaviorally what types of people they are. Generally your senior level people—your CEOs, COOs, and CIOs—will be dominant/aggressive/assertive and have good people skills.

Once I have the perceptions, realities, and personality assessments, I sit down with the president and senior level managers and talk about my comments, observations, and recommendations as they relate to the outcomes we're striving to achieve. The next step is to develop programs, systems/procedures, and accountability metrics. Sometimes I'll walk away from the prospective assignment at this point if I can't help the client or if there is a personality disconnect with the senior management team. My ultimate goal is to provide take-away value to the client, not just theory or fluff. The definition of value I apply to my work is "satisfaction greater than cost."

My typical coaching assignment is four to six months.

Wright

What a great conversation, Daniel. I've really enjoyed this and I've learned a lot. I think I'm going to run out and buy your book.

Today we have been talking with Daniel Abramson. His energetic, no-nonsense style delivers a refreshing approach to clients seeking results at a new level. His philosophy is simple. His training is tough and results, as we have found out, are rewarding. Daniel offers his uncomplicated and easy-to-follow strategies for success through speaking engagements, coaching, as well as content-rich corporate consulting. His polished delivery, contagious energy, and proven ability as a constant business strategist consistently earns him rave reviews that last well beyond his program sessions.

Daniel, thank you so much for being with us today.

About the Author

DANIEL ABRAMSON, CTS, President and Founder of Staff Dynamics, has been focused on workforce performance strategies and raising the bar for over twenty-five years. Prior to StaffDynamics, Daniel was President of an international staffing firm with over 120 offices. Under his leadership, revenues nearly tripled, and profits increased almost nine-fold, making him uniquely qualified to guide individuals and corporations in exceeding their operational and financial objectives. His energetic, no-nonsense style delivers a refreshing approach to clients seeking results at a new level. His philosophy is simple, his training is tough, his results are rewarding. Daniel offers his uncomplicated, easy-to-follow strategies for success through speaking engagements and coaching as well as content-rich corporate consulting. His polished delivery, contagious energy, and proven ability as a consummate business strategist consistently earns rave reviews that last well beyond his program sessions. Daniel earned his bachelor's degree in Marketing and has MBA credits. He is a certified instructor of Xerox Professional Selling Skills and DISC personality assessments, and has completed the Dale Carnegie program. In addition, he is a member of the National Speakers Association and the National Association of Training and Development. Daniel is also author of Secrets of Hiring Top Talent, available on Amazon.com. Daniel lives in the Washington, D.C., area with his wife, two daughters, and a bevy of pets.

Daniel Abramson
StaffDynamics
P.O. Box 711
Round Hill VA 20142
Phone: 877.568.2222
E-mail: Daniel@staffdynamics.biz
www.staffdynamics.biz